TOTAL
BASIC SKILLS
Grade 1

Table of Contents

Reading

Reading Comprehension

English

Spelling

Math

READING

Name _Andrea_

Name, Address, Phone

This book belongs to _Andrea_

I live at _££8 Vermont Ave Avenue_

The city I live in is _OCEANSIDE_

The state I live in is _ny_

My phone number is _516766 8388_

Name _____ Andrea

Review the Alphabet

Directions: Practice writing the letters.

Aa

Bb

Cc

Dd

Ee

Ff

Gg

Hh

Ii

Name __Andrea__

Review the Alphabet

Directions: Practice writing the letters.

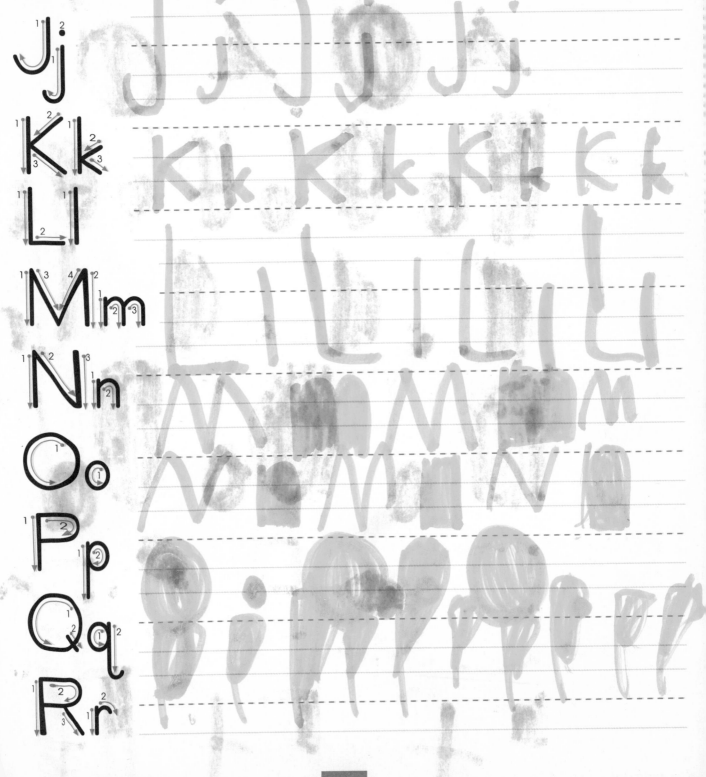

Name _____ Andrea

Review the Alphabet

Directions: Practice writing the letters.

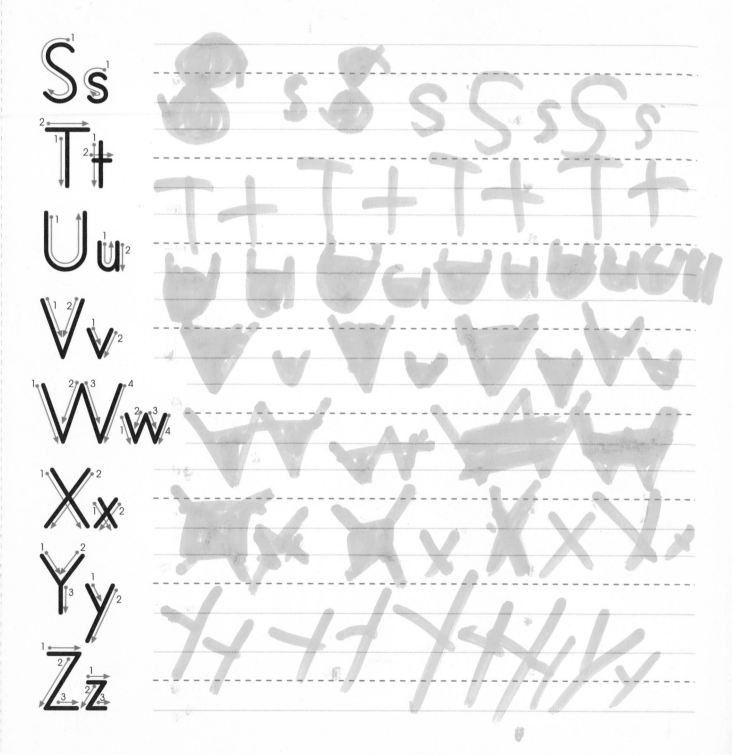

Letter Recognition

Directions: In each set, match the lower-case letter to the upper-case letter.

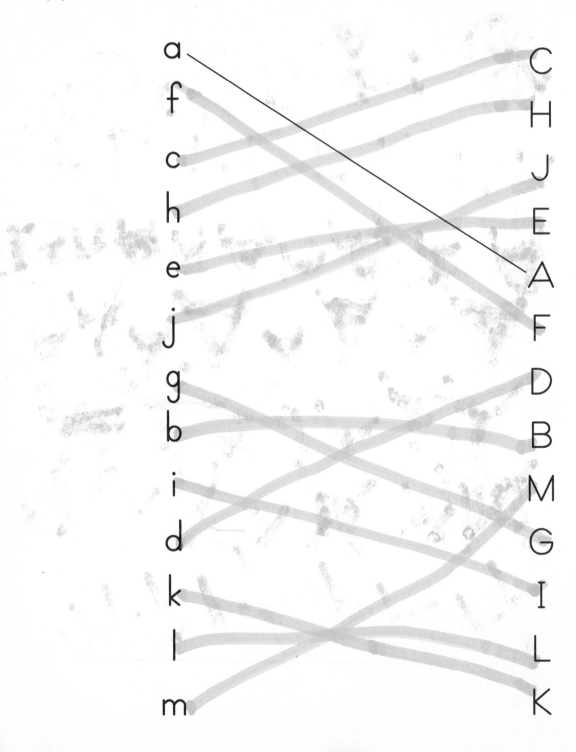

Name _Andrea_

Letter Recognition

Directions: In each set, match the lower-case letter to the upper-case letter.

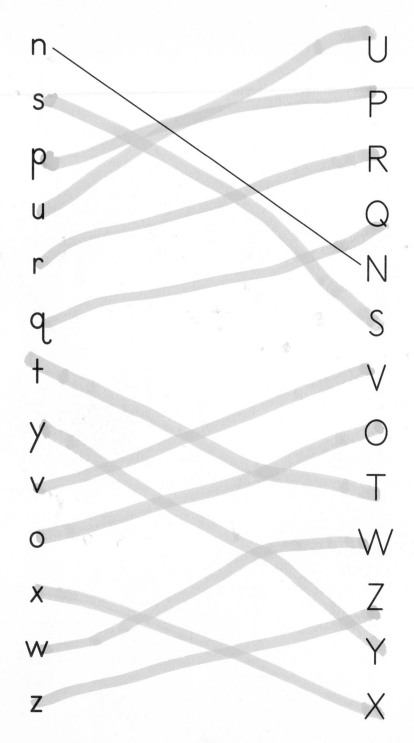

Name _Andrea_

Beginning Consonants: Bb, Cc, Dd, Ff

Beginning consonants are the sounds that come at the beginning of words. Consonants are the letters b, c, d, f, g, h, j, k, l, m, n, p, q, r, s, t, v, w, x, y and z.

Directions: Say the name of each letter. Say the sound each letter makes. Circle the letters that make the beginning sound for each picture.

Bb   Cc   Dd   Ff

Bb Dd   Ff Cc   Cc Dd   Ff Bb

Bb Dd   Ff Cc   Cc Dd   Ff Bb

Beginning Consonants: Bb, Cc, Dd, Ff

Directions: Say the name of each letter. Say the sound each letter makes. Draw a line from each letter to the picture which begins with that sound.

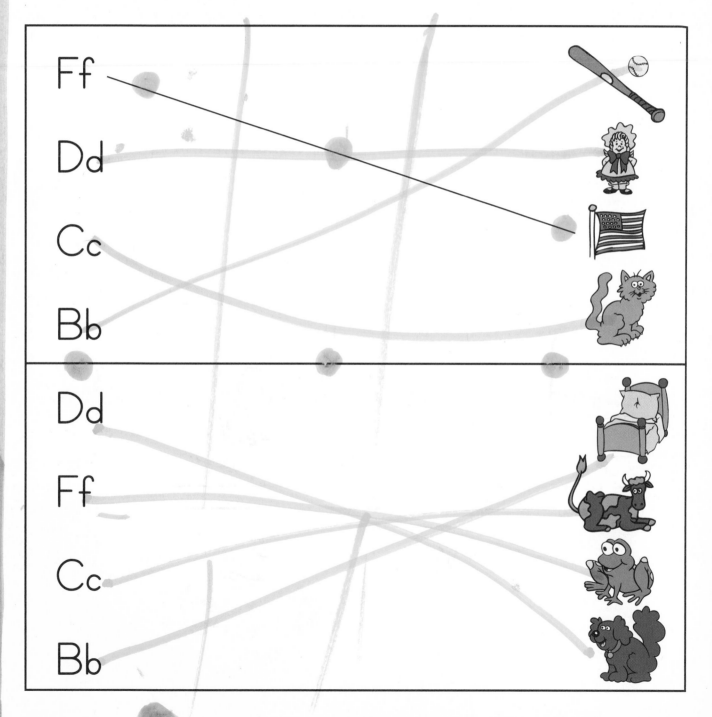

Name _Andrea_

Beginning Consonants: Gg, Hh, Jj, Kk

Directions: Say the name of each letter. Say the sound each letter makes. Trace the letter pair that makes the beginning sound in each picture.

Name _____

Beginning Consonants: Gg, Hh, Jj, Kk

Directions: Say the name of each letter. Say the sound each letter makes. Draw a line from each letter pair to the picture which begins with that sound.

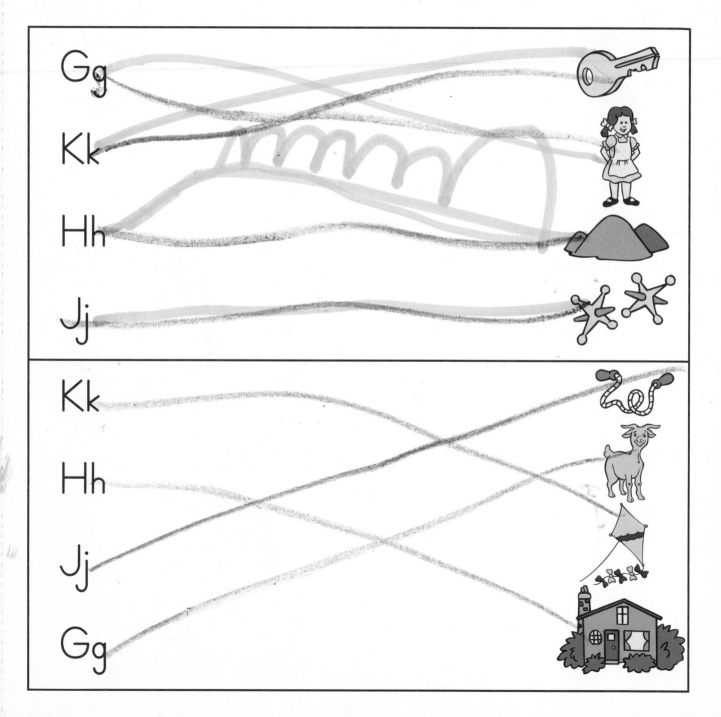

15

Name _Andred_

Beginning Consonants: Ll, Mm, Nn, Pp

Directions: Say the name of each letter. Say the sound each letter makes. Trace the letters. Then draw a line from each letter pair to the picture which begins with that sound.

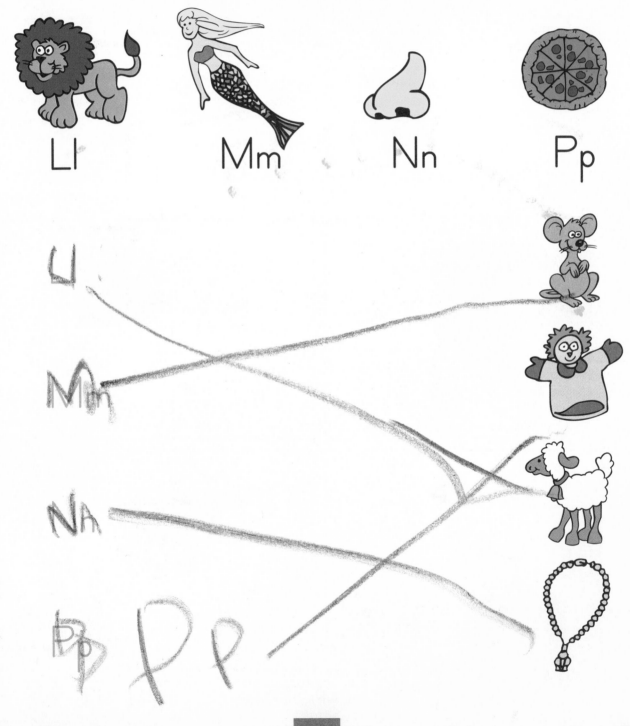

Beginning Consonants: Ll, Mm, Nn, Pp

Directions: Say the name of each letter. Say the sound each letter makes. Trace the letter pair that makes the beginning sound in each picture.

Beginning Consonants: Qq, Rr, Ss, Tt

Directions: Say the name of each letter. Say the sound each letter makes. Trace the letter pair in the boxes. Then color the picture which begins with that sound.

Name _____

Beginning Consonants: Qq, Rr, Ss, Tt

Directions: Say the name of each letter. Say the sound each letter makes. Draw a line from each letter pair to the picture which begins with that sound.

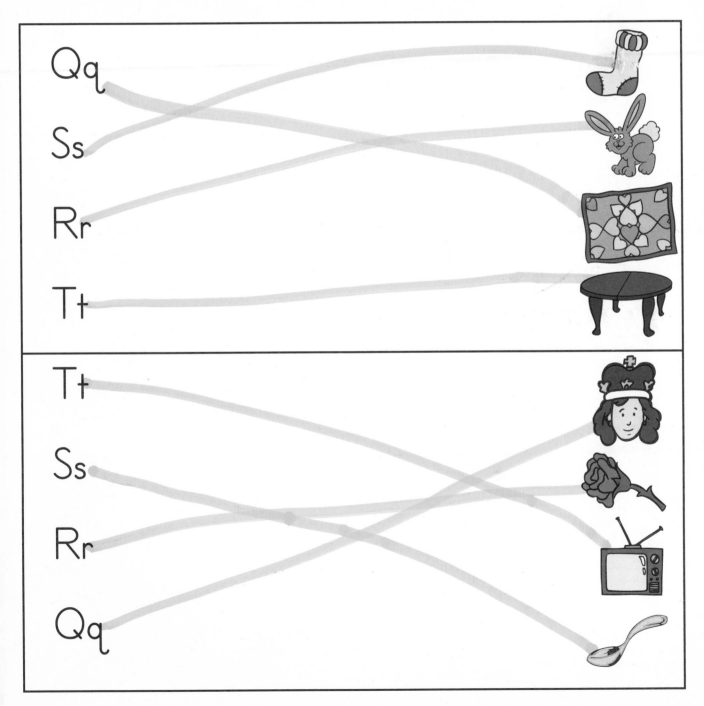

19

Name _Andrea_

Beginning Consonants: Vv, Ww, Xx, Yy, Zz

Directions: Say the name of each letter. Say the sound each letter makes. Trace the letters. Then draw a line from each letter pair to the picture which begins with that sound.

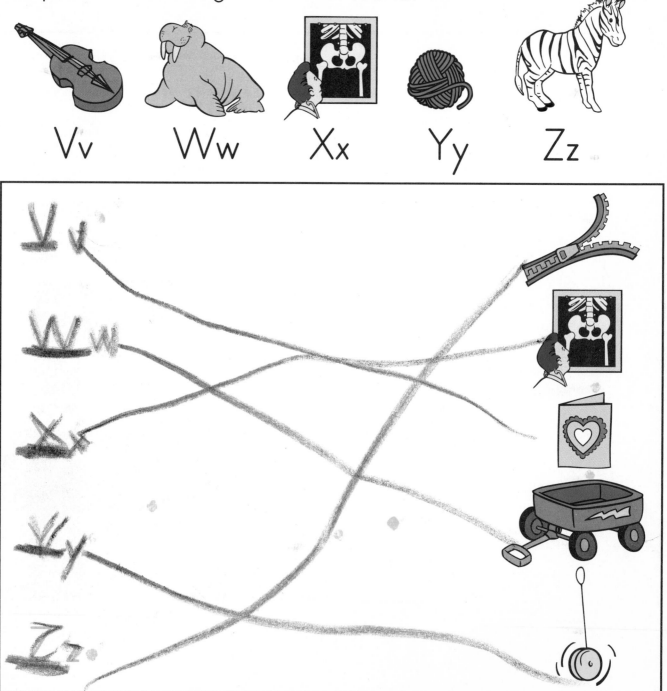

Vv   Ww   Xx   Yy   Zz

Ending Consonants: g, m, n

Directions: Say the name of each picture. Draw a line from each letter to the pictures which end with that sound.

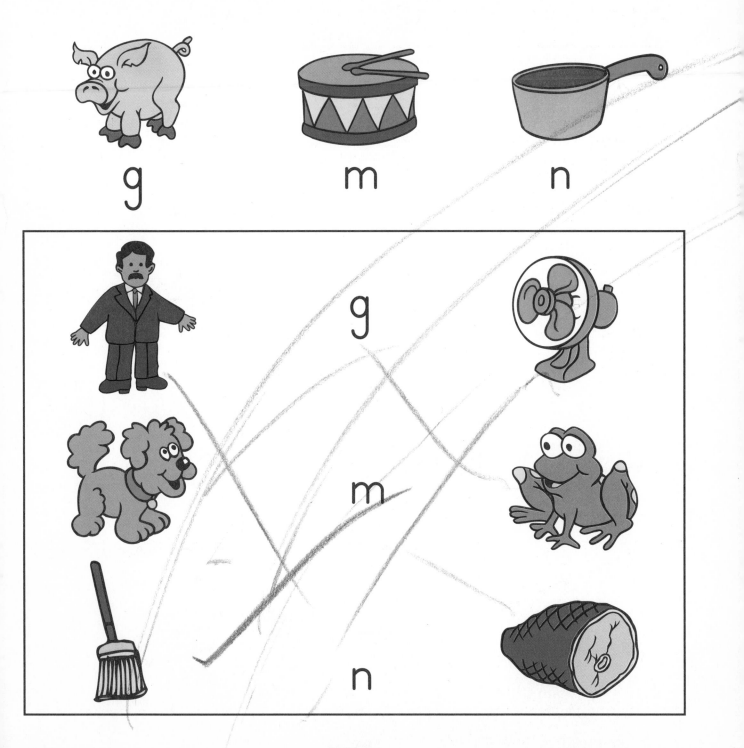

g

m

n

g

m

n

Ending Consonants: k, l, p

Directions: Trace the letters in each row. Say the name of each picture. Then color the pictures in each row which end with that sound.

Ending Consonants: r, s, t, x

Directions: Say the name of each picture. Then circle the ending sound for each picture.

r s t x   r s t x

r s t x   r s t x

r s t x   r s t x

r s t x   r s t x

Name _____

Short Vowels

Vowels are the letters **a, e, i, o** and **u**. Short **a** is the sound you hear in **ant**. Short **e** is the sound you hear in **elephant**. Short **i** is the sound you hear in **igloo**. Short **o** is the sound you hear in **octopus**. Short **u** is the sound you hear in **umbrella**.

Directions: Say the short vowel sound at the beginning of each row. Say the name of each picture. Then color the pictures which have the same short vowel sounds as that letter.

Total Basic Skills Grade 1

26

Reading

Name _____

Short Vowel Sounds

Directions: In each box are three pictures. The words that name the pictures have missing letters. Write **a, e, i, o** or **u** to finish the words.

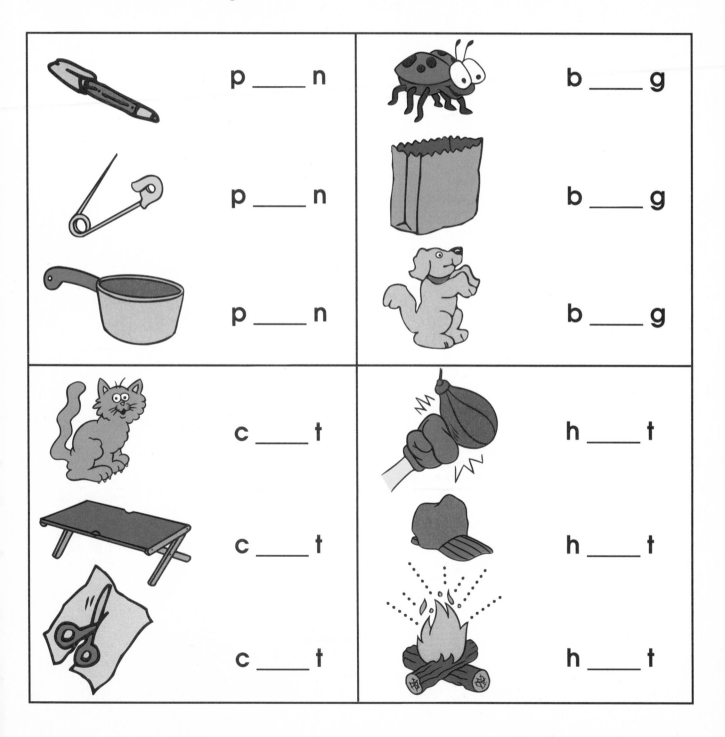

p ___ n

p ___ n

p ___ n

b ___ g

b ___ g

b ___ g

c ___ t

c ___ t

c ___ t

h ___ t

h ___ t

h ___ t

Name _____

Long Vowels

Vowels are the letters **a**, **e**, **i**, **o** and **u**. Long vowel sounds say their own names. Long **a** is the sound you hear in **hay**. Long **e** is the sound you hear in **me**. Long **i** is the sound you hear in **pie**. Long **o** is the sound you hear in **no**. Long **u** is the sound you hear in **cute**.

Directions: Say the long vowel sound at the beginning of each row. Say the name of each picture. Color the pictures in each row that have the same long vowel sound as that letter.

Long Vowel Sounds

Directions: Write **a, e, i, o** or **u** in each blank to finish the word. Draw a line from the word to the picture.

c __ ke

r __ se

k __ te

f __ t

m __ le

Words With a

Directions: Each train has a group of pictures. Write the word that names the pictures. Read your rhyming words.

These trains use the short **a** sound like in the word cat:

These trains use the long **a** sound like in the word lake:

Short and Long Aa

Directions: Say the name of each picture. If it has the short **a** sound, color it **red**. If it has the long **a** sound, color it **yellow**.

ă

ā

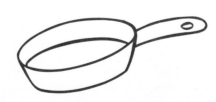

Name _____

Words With e

Directions: Short **e** sounds like the **e** in hen. Long **e** sounds like the **e** in bee. Look at the pictures. If the word has a short **e** sound, draw a line to the **hen** with your **red** crayon. If the word has a long **e** sound, draw a line to the **bee** with your **green** crayon.

hen

bee

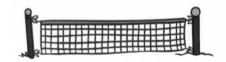

Name _____

Short and Long Ee

Directions: Say the name of each picture. Circle the pictures which have the short **e** sound. Draw a triangle around the pictures which have the long **e** sound.

ĕ

ē

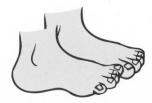

Reading

33

Total Basic Skills Grade 1

Name _____

Words With i

Directions: Short **i** sounds like the **i** in pig. Long **i** sounds like the **i** in kite. Draw a circle around the words with the short **i** sound. Draw an **X** on the words with the long **i** sound.

pin

five

pig

slide

kite

lid

tie

bib

pie

Name _____

Short and Long Ii

Directions: Say the name of each picture. If it has the short **i** sound, color it **yellow**. If it has the long **i** sound, color it **red**.

Words With o

Directions: The short **o** sounds like the **o** in dog. Long **o** sounds like the **o** in rope. Draw a line from the picture to the word that names it. Draw a circle around the word if it has a short **o** sound.

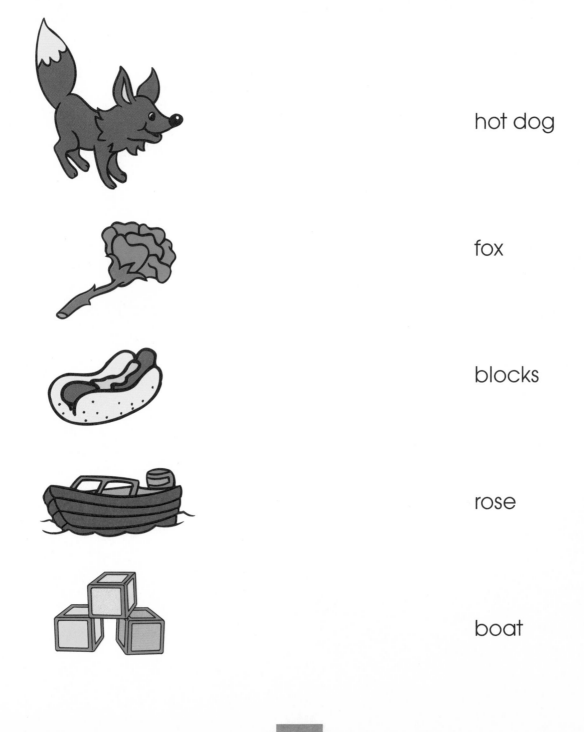

hot dog

fox

blocks

rose

boat

Name _____

Short and Long Oo

Directions: Say the name of each picture. If the picture has the long **o** sound, write a **green L** on the blank. If the picture has the short **o** sound, write a **red S** on the blank.

Words With u

Directions: The short **u** sounds like the **u** in bug. The long **u** sounds like the **u** in blue. Draw a circle around the words with short **u**. Draw an **X** on the words with long **u**.

rug

cup

music

tub

suit

glue

bug

puppy

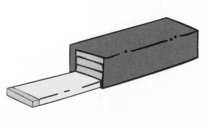

gum

Short and Long Uu

Directions: Say the name of each picture. If it has the long **u** sound, write a **u** in the **unicorn** column. If it has the short **u** sound, write a **u** in the **umbrella** column.

ū

ŭ

_____   _____

_____   _____

_____   _____

_____   _____

_____   _____

Name _____

Super Silent E

When you add an **e** to the end of some words, the vowel changes from a short vowel sound to a long vowel sound. The **e** is silent.

Example: rip + **e** = ripe.

Directions: Say the word under the first picture in each pair. Then add an **e** to the word under the next picture. Say the new word.

pet   _____

tub   _____

man   _____

kit   _____

pin   _____

cap   _____

Consonant Blends

Consonant blends are two or more consonant sounds together in a word. The blend is made by combining the consonant sounds.

Example: **fl**oor

Directions: The name of each picture begins with a **blend**. Circle the beginning blend for each picture.

bl   fl   cl

cl   fl   gl

fl   bl   pl

fl   cl   gl

pl   gl   cl

gl   fl   sl

gl   fl   cl

sl   fl   cl

cl   gl   sl

GRADE

1

Name _____

Consonant Blends

Directions: The beginning blend for each word is missing. Fill in the correct blend to finish the word. Draw a line from the word to the picture.

_ _ _ _ _ _ _ _ _ _ _ _ _ _ ain

_ _ _ _ _ _ _ _ _ _ _ _ _ _ og

_ _ _ _ _ _ _ _ _ _ _ _ _ _ ab

_ _ _ _ _ _ _ _ _ _ _ _ _ _ um

_ _ _ _ _ _ _ _ _ _ _ _ _ _ ush

_ _ _ _ _ _ _ _ _ _ _ _ _ _ esent

GRADE 1

Name _____

Consonant Blends

Directions: Draw a line from the picture to the blend that begins its word.

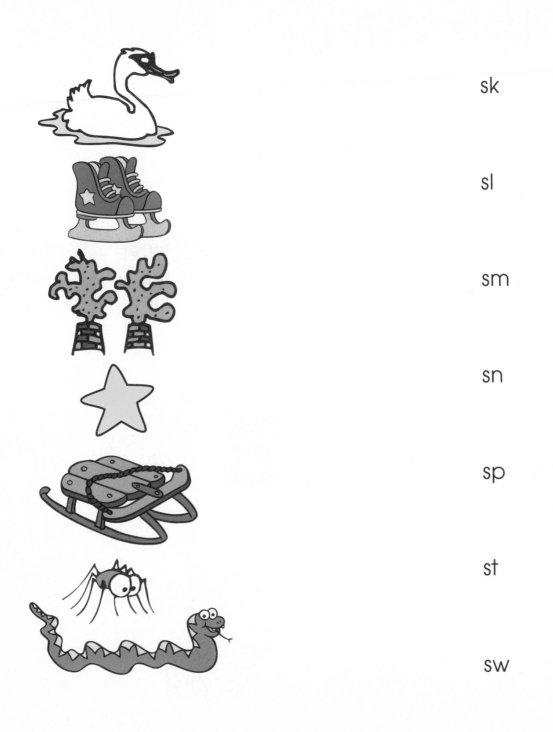

sk

sl

sm

sn

sp

st

sw

Name _____

Consonant Blends

Directions: Look at the first picture in each row. Circle the pictures in the row that begin with the same sound.

GRADE 1

Name _____

Beginning Blends

Directions: Say the blend for each word as you search for it.

b	l	o	s	l	e	d	a	b	f	t	k	a	i	n
l	b	r	e	a	d	x	s	t	o	p	i	x	a	p
o	l	g	u	f	e	n	p	s	p	i	d	e	r	i
c	l	o	w	n	a	w	l	p	z	j	c	r	a	b
k	t	c	e	n	t	h	s	t	e	g	l	q	c	r
d	h	b	r	e	a	e	j	w	k	x	o	w	h	y
h	u	s	n	a	k	e	m	d	j	l	c	m	a	j
v	m	i	u	k	l	l	s	k	u	n	k	c	i	f
i	b	g	l	o	b	e	m	h	n	o	q	t	r	r
b	f	l	j	x	s	y	a	z	s	l	e	d	o	o
s	h	e	l	l	w	k	l	f	s	s	v	u	p	g
h	a	r	l	c	a	d	l	l	v	w	k	z	s	n
o	z	y	q	s	n	l	t	a	h	n	r	u	m	q
e	f	l	o	w	e	r	a	g	l	o	v	e	e	r
w	g	m	b	c	e	n	m	o	p	d	o	f	l	g
p	r	e	s	e	n	t	r	a	i	n	b	p	l	i

Words to find:

block	sled	globe	crab
clock	frog	present	flower
train	glove	skunk	snake
swan	flag	smell	spider
bread	small	chair	shell
stop	sled	shoe	
thumb	wheel	clown	

Reading

45

Total Basic Skills Grade 1

Ending Consonant Blends

Directions: Write **lt** or **ft** to complete the words.

be _____

ra _____

sa _____

qui _____

le _____

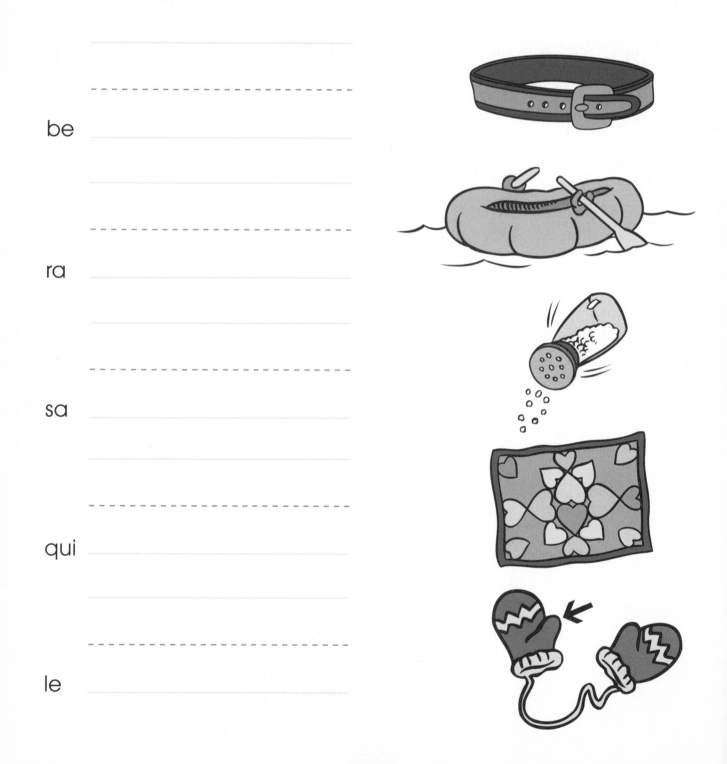

Name _____

Ending Consonant Blends

Directions: Draw a line from the picture to the blend that ends the word.

lf

lk

sk

st

47

Name _____

Ending Consonant Blends

Directions: Every juke box has a word ending and a list of letters. Add each of the letters to the word ending to make rhyming words.

___and
b _____
h _____
l _____
s _____

___ent
b _____
d _____
t _____
w _____

___ump
b _____
d _____
j _____
p _____

___ink
p _____
s _____
l _____
th _____

___ing
r _____
s _____
st _____
k _____

___ank
b _____
r _____
s _____
t _____

Ending Consonant Blends

Directions: Say the blend for each word as you search for it.

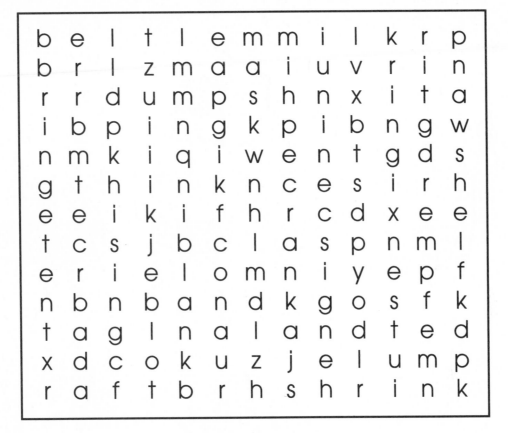

```
b  e  l  t  l  e  m  m  i  l  k  r  p
b  r  l  z  m  a  a  i  u  v  r  i  n
r  r  d  u  m  p  s  h  n  x  i  t  a
i  b  p  i  n  g  k  p  i  b  n  g  w
n  m  k  i  q  i  w  e  n  t  g  d  s
g  t  h  i  n  k  n  c  e  s  i  r  h
e  e  i  k  i  f  h  r  c  d  x  e  e
t  c  s  j  b  c  l  a  s  p  n  m  l
e  r  i  e  l  o  m  n  i  y  e  p  f
n  b  n  b  a  n  d  k  g  o  s  f  k
t  a  g  l  n  a  l  a  n  d  t  e  d
x  d  c  o  k  u  z  j  e  l  u  m  p
r  a  f  t  b  r  h  s  h  r  i  n  k
```

Words to find:

belt	raft	milk	shelf
mask	clasp	nest	band
think	went	lump	crank
ring	blank	shrink	land
bring	tent	dump	sing

Rhyming Words

Rhyming words are words that sound alike at the end of the word. **Cat** and **hat** rhyme.

Directions: Draw a circle around each word pair that rhymes. Draw an **X** on each pair that does not rhyme.

Example:

soap
rope

red
dog

book
hook

cold
rock

cat
hat

yellow
black

one
two

rock
sock

rat
flat

good
nice

you
to

meet
toy

old
sold

sale
whale

word
letter

Rhyming Words

Rhyming words are words that sound alike at the end of the word.

Directions: Draw a line to match the pictures that rhyme. Write two of your rhyming word pairs below.

-          -

-          -

Name _____

ABC Order

Directions: Abc order is the order in which letters come in the alphabet. Draw a line to connect the dots. Follow the letters in **abc** order. Then color the picture.

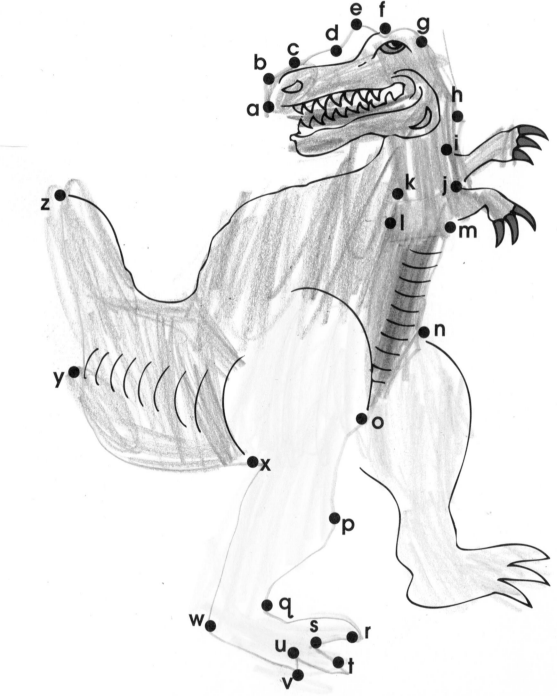

Name _Andrea_

ABC Order

Directions: Draw a line to connect the dots. Follow the letters in abc order. Then color the picture.

Name _____

ABC Order

Directions: Circle the first letter of each word. Then put each pair of the words in abc order.

ⓒar   ⓑird   moon   two   nest   fan

bird

car

card   dog   pig   bike   sun   pie

Name _____

ABC Order

Directions: Look at the words in each box. Circle the word that comes first in abc order.

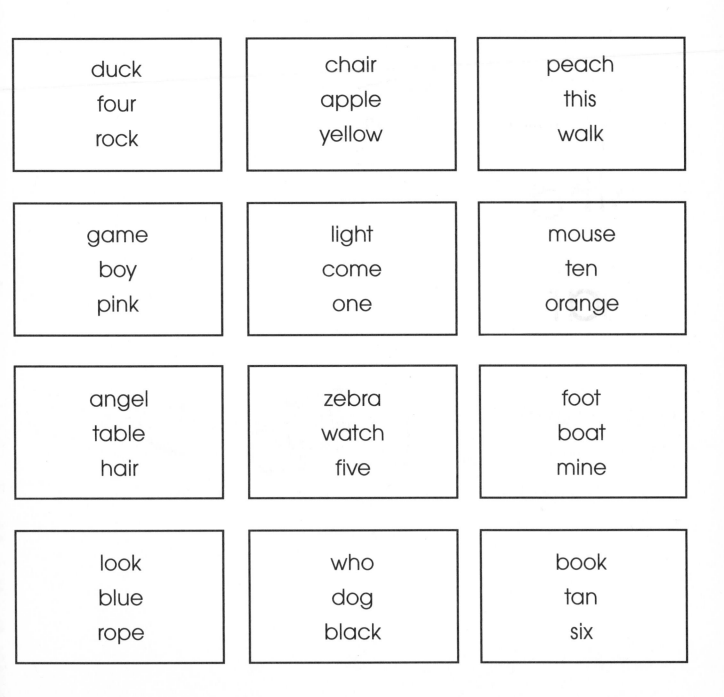

duck four rock	chair apple yellow	peach this walk
game boy pink	light come one	mouse ten orange
angel table hair	zebra watch five	foot boat mine
look blue rope	who dog black	book tan six

Name _____

Compound Words

Compound words are two words that are put together to make one new word.

Directions: Look at the pictures and the two words that are next to each other. Put the words together to make a new word. Write the new word.

Example:

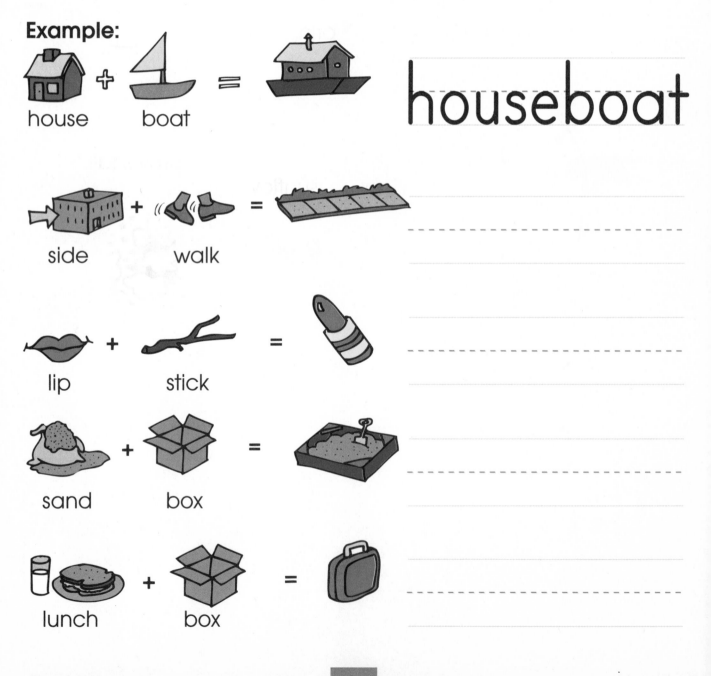

house + boat = houseboat

side + walk = _____

lip + stick = _____

sand + box = _____

lunch + box = _____

Compound Words

Directions: Circle the compound word which completes each sentence. Write each word on the lines.

1. The _____ brings us letters.

      mailman   snowman

2. A _____ grows tall.

      sunlight   sunflower

3. The snow falls _____.

      outside   inside

4. A _____ fell on my head.

      raindrop   rainbow

5. I put the letter in a _____.

      mailbox   shoebox

Names

You are a special person. Your name begins with a capital letter. We put a capital letter at the beginning of people's names because they are special.

Directions: Write your name. Did you remember to use a capital letter?

_____

- -

_____

Directions: Write each person's name. Use a capital letter at the beginning.

Ted — -

Katie — -

Mike — -

Tim — -

Write a friend's name. Use a capital letter at the beginning.

- -

Names: Days of the Week

The days of the week begin with capital letters.

Directions: Write the days of the week in the spaces below. Put them in order. Be sure to start with capital letters.

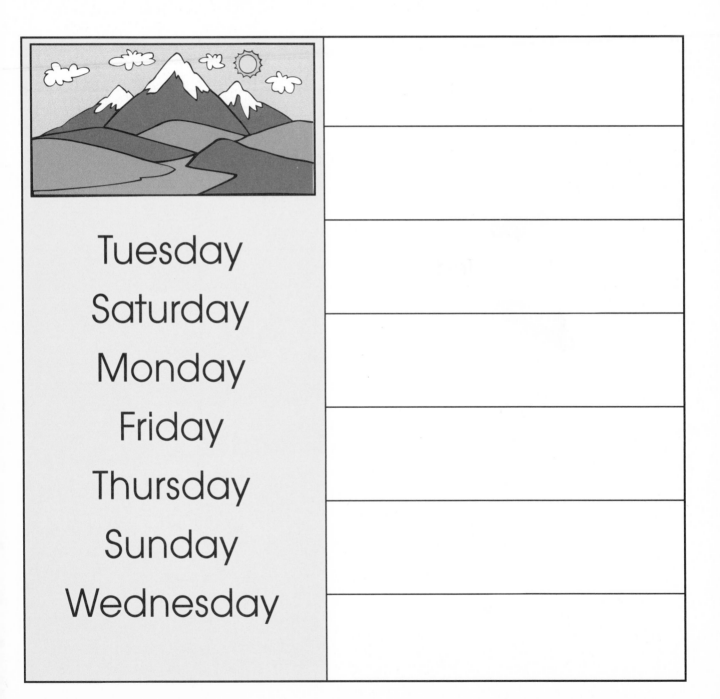

Tuesday

Saturday

Monday

Friday

Thursday

Sunday

Wednesday

Name _____

Names: Months of the Year

The months of the year begin with capital letters.

Directions: Write the months of the year in order on the calendar below. Be sure to use capital letters.

January	December	April	May	October	June
September	February	July	March	November	August

Name _____

More Than One

Directions: An **s** at the end of a word often means there is more than one. Look at each picture. Circle the correct word. Write the word on the line.

two
dog   dogs

- - - - - - - - - - - - -

four
flower   flowers

- - - - - - - - - - - - -

one
bikes   bike

- - - - - - - - - - - - -

three
toys   toy

- - - - - - - - - - - - -

a
lamb   lambs

- - - - - - - - - - - - -

two
cat   cats

- - - - - - - - - - - - -

More Than One

Directions: Read the nouns under the pictures. Then write each noun under **One** or **More Than One**.

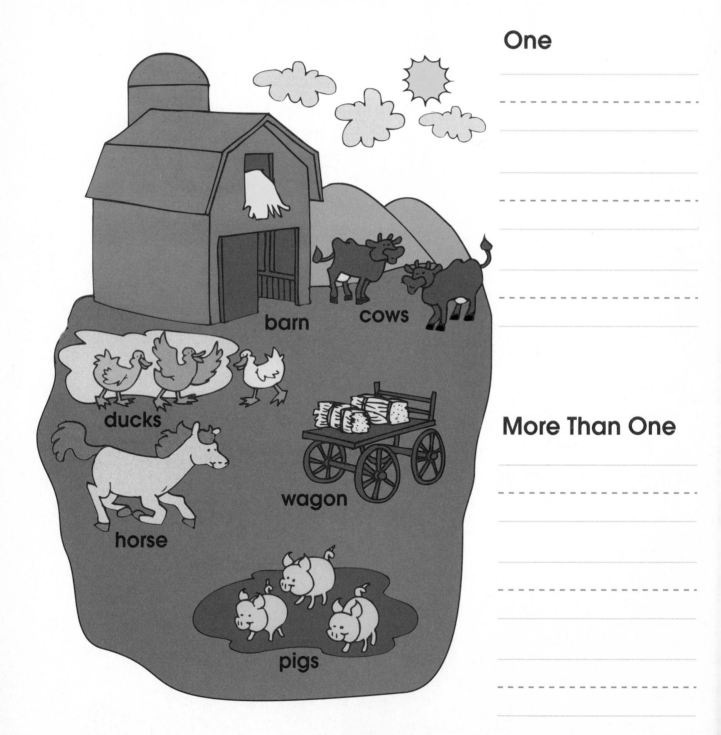

barn

cows

ducks

wagon

horse

pigs

One

More Than One

READING COMPREHENSION

Name _____

More Than One

Directions: Choose the word which completes each sentence. Write each word on the line.

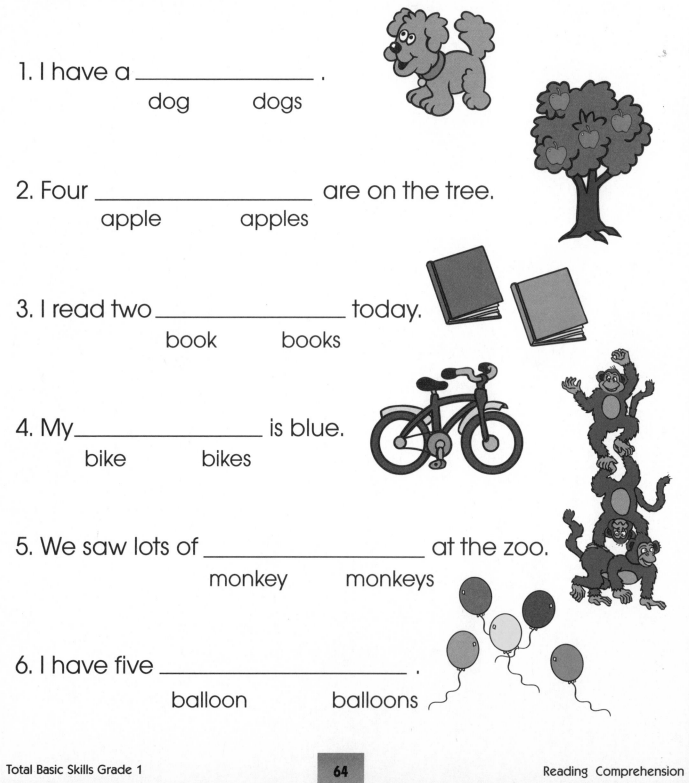

1. I have a _____ .

    dog   dogs

2. Four _____ are on the tree.

    apple   apples

3. I read two _____ today.

    book   books

4. My _____ is blue.

    bike   bikes

5. We saw lots of _____ at the zoo.

    monkey   monkeys

6. I have five _____ .

    balloon   balloons

Riddles

Directions: Read the word. Trace and write it on the line. Then draw a line from the riddle to the animal it tells about.

long **long**

I am very big.
I lived a long, long time ago.
What am I?

giraffe

My neck is very long.
I eat leaves from trees.
What am I?

rabbit

I have long ears.
I hop very fast.
What am I?

dinosaur

Name _____

Riddles

Directions: Read the word and write it on the line. Then read each riddle and draw a line to the picture and word that tells about it.

house

_____

I like to play.
I am little. I am soft.
What am I?

house

kitten

_____

I am big.
You live in me.
What am I?

kitten

flower

_____

I am pretty.
I am green and yellow.
What am I?

flower

pony

_____

I can jump. I can run.
I am brown.
What am I?

pony

Riddles

Directions: Write a word from the box to answer each riddle.

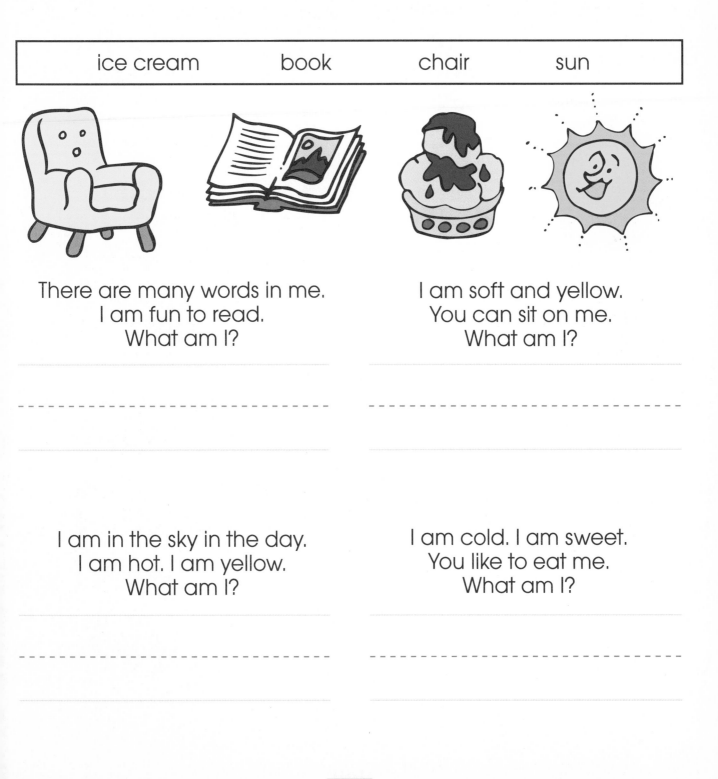

| ice cream | book | chair | sun |

There are many words in me.
I am fun to read.
What am I?

_____

_____

I am soft and yellow.
You can sit on me.
What am I?

_____

_____

I am in the sky in the day.
I am hot. I am yellow.
What am I?

_____

_____

I am cold. I am sweet.
You like to eat me.
What am I?

_____

_____

Picture Clues

Directions: Read the sentence. Circle the word that makes sense. Use the picture clues to help you. Then write the word.

I ride on a _____ .
bike   hike

I ride on a _____ .
train   tree

I ride in a _____ .
car   can

I ride on a _____ .
bus   bug

I ride in a _____ .
jar   jet

I ride in a _____ .
took   truck

Name _____

Picture Clues

Directions: Read the sentence. Circle the word that makes sense. Use the picture clues to help you. Then write the word.

I see the _____ .

bird   book

I see the _____ .

fish   fork

I see the _____ .

dogs   dig

I see the _____ .

cats   coat

I see the _____ .

snake   snow

I see the _____ .

rat   rake

Name _____

Comprehension

Directions: Look at the picture. Write the words from the box to finish the sentences.

frog	log	bird	fish	ducks

The _____ can jump.

The turtle is on a _____ .

A _____ is in the tree.

The boy wants a _____ .

I see three _____ .

Comprehension

Directions: Read the poem. Write the correct words in the blanks.

A Poem

The hat was on a mat.
A cat sat on the hat.
Now the hat is flat.

The hat was on _____ .

Who sat on the hat? _____

Now the hat is _____ .

Following Directions: Color the Path

Directions: Color the path the girl should take to go home. Use the sentences to help you.

1. Go to the school and turn left.

2. At the end of the street, turn right.

3. Walk past the park and turn right.

4. After you pass the pool, turn right.

Name _____

Following Directions

Directions: Look at the pictures. Follow the directions in each box.

Draw a circle around the caterpillar.
Draw a line under the stick.

Draw an **X** on the mother bird.
Draw a triangle around the baby birds.

Draw a box around the rabbit.

Color the flowers. Count the bees.
There are _____ bees.

Classifying

Directions: Classifying is sorting things into groups. Draw a circle around the pictures that answer the question.

What Can Swim?

What Can Fly?

Classifying: These Keep Me Warm

Directions: Color the things that keep you warm.

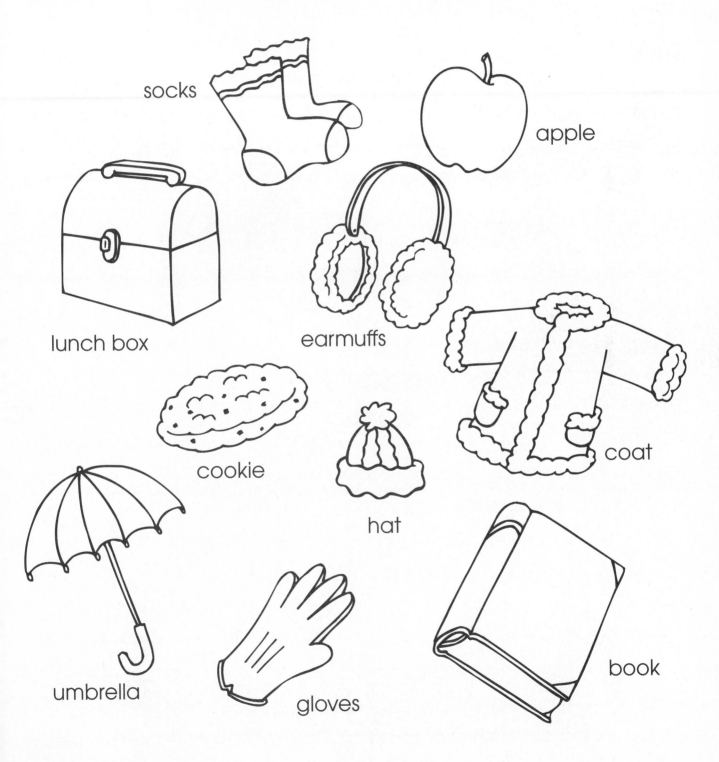

socks

apple

lunch box

earmuffs

cookie

coat

hat

umbrella

gloves

book

Name _____

Classifying: Objects

Help Dan clean up the park.

Directions: Circle the litter. Underline the coins. Draw a box around the balls.

Name _____

Classifying: Things to Drink

Directions: Circle the pictures of things you can drink. Write the names of those things in the blanks.

milk

ice

soup and crackers

juice

soda

ice-cream bar

Name _____

Vocabulary

Directions: Read the words. Trace and write them on the lines. Look at each picture. Write **hot** or **cold** on the lines to show if it is hot or cold.

hot　　　hot

cold　　cold

Name _____

Vocabulary

Directions: Read the words. Trace and write them on the lines. Look at each picture and write **day** or **night** on the lines to show if they happen during the day or night.

day   day

night   night

Classifying: Night and Day

Directions: Write the words from the box under the pictures they describe.

| stars   sun   moon   rays   dark   light   night   day |

Classifying: Clowns and Balloons

Some words describe clowns. Some words describe balloons.

Directions: Read the words. Write the words that match in the correct columns.

float	laughs	hat	string
air	feet	pop	nose

clown

balloons

Name _____

Similarities: Objects

Directions: Circle the picture in each row that is most like the first picture.

Example:

| potato | rose | tomato | tree |

| shirt | mittens | boots | jacket |

| whale | cat | dolphin | monkey |

| tiger | giraffe | lion | zebra |

Name _____

Similarities: Objects

Directions: Circle the picture in each row that is most like the first picture.

Example:

| carrot | jacks | bread | pea |

| baseball | sneakers | basketball | bat |

| store | school | home | bakery |

| kitten | dog | fox | cat |

Name _____

Classifying: Food Groups

Directions: Color the meats and eggs brown. Color the fruits and vegetables green. Color the breads tan. Color the dairy foods (milk and cheese) yellow.

fish   bread   apple   cheese

crackers   carrot   orange   eggs

steaks   pear   milk   yogurt

ice cream   chicken   potato   pretzel

Name _____

Same and Different: These Don't Belong

Directions: Circle the pictures in each row that go together.

Row 1   cookies   cake   beans   ice cream

Row 2   apple   banana   orange   cookies

Row 3   kite   dice   checkers   chess

Directions: Write the names of the things that do not belong.

Row 1 _____

Row 2 _____

Row 3 _____

Name _____

Classifying: What Does Not Belong?

Directions: Draw an **X** on the picture that does not belong in each group.

fruit

| apple | peach | corn | watermelon |

wild animals

| bear | kitten | gorilla | lion |

pets

| cat | fish | elephant | dog |

flowers

| grass | rose | daisy | tulip |

Classifying: What Does Not Belong?

Directions: Draw an **X** on the word in each row that does not belong.

1.	flashlight	candle	radio	fire
2.	shirt	pants	coat	bat
3.	cow	car	bus	train
4.	beans	hot dog	ball	bread
5.	gloves	hat	book	boots
6.	fork	butter	cup	plate
7.	book	ball	bat	milk
8.	dogs	bees	flies	ants

Classifying: Objects

Directions: Write each word in the correct row at the bottom of the page.

airplane   drum   radio   plate   car   pencil

spoon   crayon   chalk   fork   television   boat

Things we ride in:

_____

- -

_____

Things we eat with:

_____

- -

_____

Things we draw with:

_____

- -

_____

Things we listen to:

_____

- -

_____

Name _____

Classifying: Names, Numbers, Animals, Colors

Directions: Write the words from the box next to the words they describe.

Joe	cat	blue	Tim
two	dog	red	ten
Sue	green	pig	six

Name
Words

_____

Number
Words

_____

Animal
Words

_____

Color
Words

_____

Name _____

Classifying: Things That Belong Together

Directions: Circle the pictures in each row that belong together.

Row 1   knife   key   fork   spoon

Row 2   orange   apple   candy   banana

Row 3   beach ball   soccer ball   baseball   apple

Directions: Write the names of the pictures that do not belong.

Row 1

- -

Row 2

- -

Row 3

Classifying: Why They Are Different

Directions: Look at your answers on page 90. Write why each object does not belong.

_____

- -

Row 1 _____

_____

- -

Row 2 _____

_____

- -

Row 3 _____

Directions: For each object, draw a group of pictures that belong with it.

candy bar _____

lettuce

Classifying: What Does Not Belong?

Directions: Circle the two things that do not belong in the picture. Write why they do not belong.

1. -

- -

- -

2. -

- -

Name _____

Sequencing: Fill the Glasses

Directions: Follow the instructions to fill each glass. Use crayons to draw your favorite drink in the ones that are full and half-full.

full **half-full** **empty**

empty **half-full** **full**

Sequencing: Raking Leaves

Directions: Write a number in each box to show the order of the story.

Sequencing: Make a Snowman!

Directions: Write the number of the sentence that goes with each picture in the box.

1. Roll a large snowball for the snowman's bottom.

2. Make another snowball and put it on top of the first.

3. Put the last snowball on top.

4. Dress the snowman.

Name _____

Sequencing: A Recipe

Directions: Look at the recipe below. Put each step in order. Write **1, 2, 3** or **4** in the box.

HOW TO MAKE BREAD BUDDIES

Roll dough into balls and shapes. Connect pieces with a drop of water.

Mix 1 cup of water, 1 cup of salt and 3 cups of flour.

Knead the dough.

Have an adult bake your bread buddy for 2-3 hours at 300°. Let it cool. Then paint it!

What kind of bread buddy did you make?

_____

- -

_____

Name _____

Sequencing: How Flowers Grow

Directions: Read the story. Then write the steps to grow a flower.

First find a sunny spot. Then plant the seed. Water it. The flower will start to grow. Pull the weeds around it. Remember to keep giving the flower water. Enjoy your flower.

1. _____ .

2. _____ .

3. _____ .

4. _____ .

5. _____ .

Comprehension: Apples

Directions: Read about apples. Then write the answers.

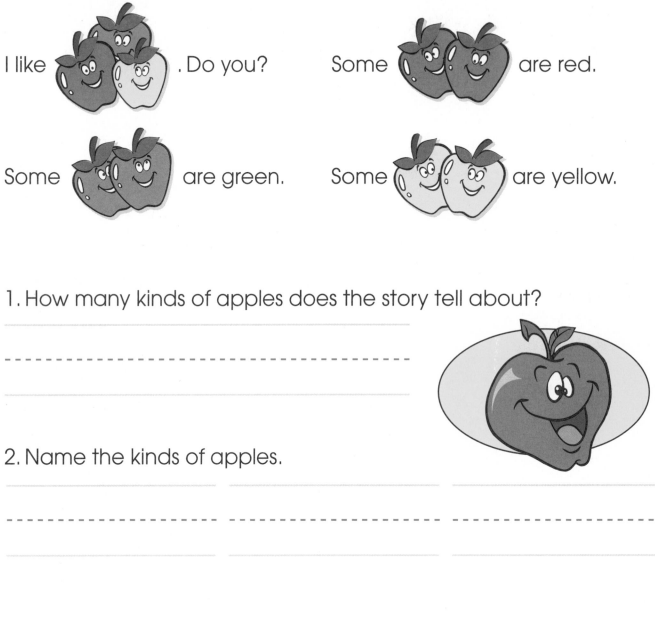

I like [apples]. Do you?

Some [apples] are red.

Some [apples] are green.

Some [apples] are yellow.

1. How many kinds of apples does the story tell about?

- -

2. Name the kinds of apples.

- -

3. What kind of apple do you like best?

- -

Name _____

Comprehension: Crayons

Directions: Read about crayons. Then write your answers.

Crayons come in many colors.
Some crayons are dark colors.
Some crayons are light colors.
All crayons have wax in them.

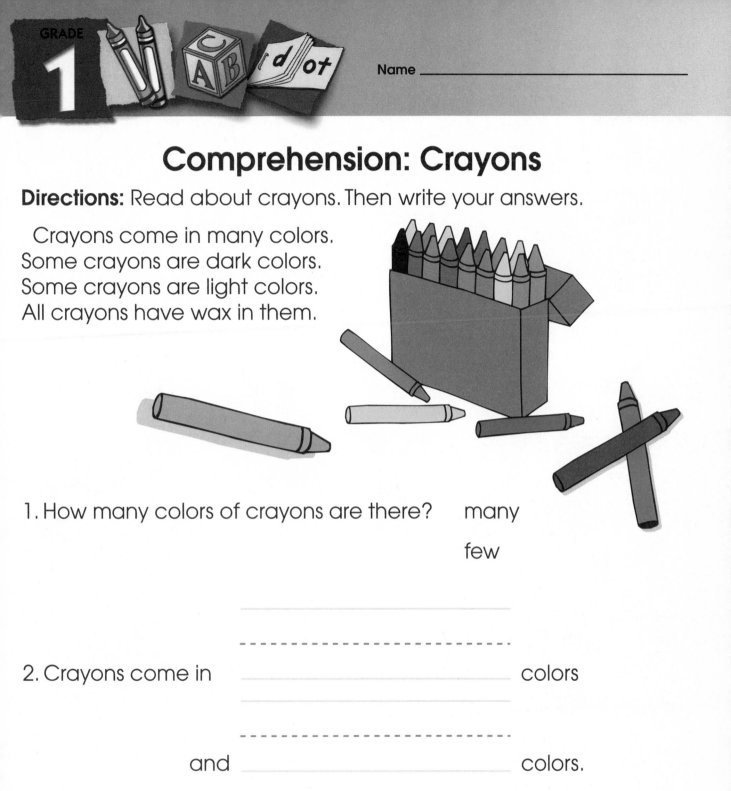

1. How many colors of crayons are there?   many

     few

2. Crayons come in _____ colors

and _____ colors.

3. What do all crayons have in them?

_____

_____

Name _____

Comprehension

Directions: Read the story. Write the words from the story that complete each sentence.

Jane and Bill like to play in the rain. They take off their shoes and socks.
They splash in the puddles.
It feels cold!
It is fun to splash!

Jane and Bill like to _____ .

They take off their _____ .

They splash in _____ .

Do you like to splash in puddles?   Yes   No

Name _____

Comprehension

Directions: Read the story. Write the words from the story that complete each sentence.

Ben and Sue have a bug.
It is red with black spots.
They call it Spot.
Spot likes to eat green
leaves and grass.
The children keep Spot in a box.

_____

Ben and Sue have a _____ .

It is _____ with black spots.

The bug's name is _____ .

The bug eats _____ .

GRADE 1

Name _____

Comprehension: Growing Flowers

Directions: Read about flowers. Then write the answers.

Some flowers grow in pots. Many flowers grow in flower beds. Others grow beside the road. Flowers begin from seeds. They grow into small buds. Then they open wide and bloom. Flowers are pretty!

1. Name two places flowers grow.

_____

_____

2. Flowers begin from _____ .

3. Then flowers grow into small _____ .

4. Flowers then open wide and _____ .

Comprehension: Raking Leaves

Directions: Read about raking leaves. Then answer the questions.

I like to rake leaves. Do you? Leaves die each year. They get brown and dry. They fall from the trees. Then we rake them up.

1. What color are leaves when they die?

_____

2. What happens when they die?

_____

_____

_____

3. What do we do when leaves fall?

_____

Comprehension: Clocks

Directions: Read about clocks. Then answer the questions.

Ticking Clocks

Many clocks make two sounds. The sounds are tick and tock. Big clocks often make loud tick-tocks. Little clocks often make quiet tick-tocks. Sometimes people put little clocks in a box with a new puppy. The puppy likes the sound. The tick-tock makes the puppy feel safe.

1. What two sounds do many clocks make?

_____   _____

and _____

2. What kind of tick-tocks do big clocks make?

_____

_____

3. What kind of clock makes a new puppy feel safe?

_____

_____

Name _____

Comprehension: Soup

Directions: Read about soup. Then write the answers.

I Like Soup

Soup is good! It is good for you, too. We eat most kinds of soup hot. Some people eat cold soup in the summer. Carrots and beans are in some soups. Do you like crackers with soup?

1. Name two ways people eat soup.

- -

2. Name two things that are in some soups.

- -

3. Name the kind of soup you like best.

- -

Name _____

Comprehension: The Teddy Bear Song

Do you know the Teddy Bear Song? It is very old!

Directions: Read the Teddy Bear Song. Then answer the questions.

Teddy bear, teddy bear, turn around.

Teddy bear, teddy bear, touch the ground.

Teddy bear, teddy bear, climb upstairs.

Teddy bear, teddy bear, say your prayers.

Teddy bear, teddy bear, turn out the light.

Teddy bear, teddy bear, say, "Good night!"

1. What is the first thing the teddy bear does?

_____

_____

2. What is the last thing the teddy bear does?

_____

_____

3. What would you name a teddy bear?

_____

_____

Sequencing: Put Teddy Bear to Bed

Directions: Read the song about the teddy bear again. Write a number in each box to show the order of the story.

Comprehension: A New Teddy Bear Song

Directions: Write words to make a new teddy bear song. Act out your new song with your teddy bear as you read it.

Teddy bear, teddy bear, turn _____ .

Teddy bear, teddy bear, touch the _____ .

Teddy bear, teddy bear, climb _____ .

Teddy bear, teddy bear, turn out _____ .

Teddy bear, teddy bear, say, _____ .

Name _____

Sequencing: Petting a Cat

Directions: Read the story. Then write the answers.

Do you like cats? I do. To pet a cat, move slowly. Hold out your hand. The cat will come to you. Then pet its head. Do not grab a cat! It will run away.

To pet a cat . . .

_____

1. Move _____ .

_____

2. Hold out your _____ .

_____

3. The cat will come to _____ .

_____

4. Pet the cat's _____ .

_____

5. Do not _____ a cat!

Name _____

Comprehension: Cats

Directions: Read the story about cats again. Then write the answers.

1. What is a good title for the story?

   _____

   - - - - - - - - - - - - - - - - - -

   _____

   - - - - - - - - - - - - - - - - - -

2. The story tells you how to _____ .

3. What part of your body should you pet a cat with?

   _____

   - - - - - - - - - - - - - - - - - - -

   _____

4. Why should you move slowly to pet a cat?

   _____

   - - - - - - - - - - - - - - - - - -

   _____ .

5. Why do you think a cat will run away if you grab it?

   _____

   - - - - - - - - - - - - - - -

   _____

   _____

   - - - - - - - - - - - - - - - .

Name _____

Comprehension: Cats

Directions: Look at the pictures and read about four cats. Then write the correct name beside each cat.

Fluffy, Blackie and Tiger are playing. Tom is sleeping. Blackie has spots. Tiger has stripes.

111

Same and Different: Cats

Directions: Compare the picture of the cats on page 149 to this picture. Write a word from the box to tell what is different about each cat.

| purple ball | green bow | blue brush | red collar |

1. Tom is wearing a _____ .

2. Blackie has a _____ .

3. Fluffy is wearing a _____ .

4. Tiger has a _____ .

Comprehension: Tigers

Directions: Read about tigers. Then write the answers.

Tigers sleep during the day. They hunt at night. Tigers eat meat. They hunt deer. They like to eat wild pigs. If they cannot find meat, tigers will eat fish.

1. When do tigers sleep?

- -

2. Name two things tigers eat.

- -

3. When do tigers hunt?

Name _____

Following Directions: Tiger Puzzle

Directions: Read the story about tigers again. Then complete the puzzle.

Across:

1. When tigers cannot get meat, they eat _____ .

3. The food tigers like best is _____ .

4. Tigers like to eat this meat: wild _____ .

Down:

2. Tigers do this during the day.

Following Directions: Draw a Tiger

Directions: Follow directions to complete the picture of the tiger.

1. Draw black stripes on the tiger's body and tail.

2. Color the tiger's tongue red.

3. Draw claws on the feet.

4. Draw a black nose and two black eyes on the tiger's face.

5. Color the rest of the tiger orange.

6. Draw tall, green grass for the tiger to sleep in.

Comprehension: Write a Party Invitation

Directions: Read about the party. Then complete the invitation.

The party will be at Dog's house. The party will start at 1:00 P.M. It will last 2 hours. Write your birthday for the date of the party.

Party Invitation

Where: _____

Date: _____

Time It Begins: _____

Time It Ends: _____

_____

Directions: On the last line, write something else about the party.

Sequencing: Pig Gets Ready

Directions: Number the pictures of Pig getting ready for the party to show the order of the story.

What kind of party do you think Pig is going to?

Comprehension: An Animal Party

Directions: Use the picture for clues. Write words from the box to answer the questions.

bear	cat
dog	elephant
giraffe	hippo
pig	tiger

1. Which animals have bow ties?

_____   _____

2. Which animal has a hat?

_____

3. Which animal has a striped shirt?

Classifying: Party Items

Directions: Draw a ☐ around objects that are food for the party. Draw a △ around the party guests. Draw a ◯ around the objects used for fun at the party.

ice cream

candy

games

tiger

noise makers

cake

garbage can

cat

hat

glasses

candle

bear

juice

balloons

giraffe

pig

potato chips

hippo

Comprehension: Rhymes

Directions: Read about words that rhyme. Then circle the answers.

Words that rhyme have the same end sounds. "Wing" and "sing" rhyme. "Boy" and "toy" rhyme. "Dime" and "time" rhyme. Can you think of other words that rhyme?

1. Words that rhyme have the same   end sounds.

          end letters.

TREE, SEE
SHOE, BLUE
KITE, BITE
MAKE, TAKE
FLY, BUY

2. Time rhymes with   "tree."

          "dime."

Directions: Write one rhyme for each word.

wing

boy

dime

pink

Name _____

Rhyming Words

Many poems have rhyming words. The rhyming words are usually at the end of the line.

Directions: Complete the poem with words from the box.

My Glue

I spilled my _____ .

I felt _____ .

What could I _____ ?

Hey! I have a _____ !

I'll make it _____ ;

The cleanest you've _____ .

No one will _____ .

Wouldn't that be _____ ?

| blue | clue | scream | seen |
| glue | do | clean | mean |

Name _____

Classifying: Rhymes

Directions: Circle the pictures in each row that rhyme.

Row 1

Row 2

Row 3

Directions: Write the names of the pictures that do not rhyme.

These words do not rhyme:

Row 1   Row 2   Row 3

_____   _____   _____

- - - - - - - - - -   - - - - - - - - - -   - - - - - - - - - -

_____   _____   _____

Predicting: Words and Pictures

Directions: Complete each story by choosing the correct picture. Draw a line from the story to the picture.

1. Shawnda got her books. She went

   to the bus stop. Shawnda got

   on the bus.

2. Marco planted a seed. He watered it.

   He pulled the weeds around it.

3. Abraham's dog was barking.

   Abraham got out the dog food.

   He put it in the dog bowl.

Predicting: Story Ending

Directions: Read the story. Draw a picture in the last box to complete the story.

That's my ball.   I got it first.

It's mine!

Name _____

Predicting: Story Ending

Directions: Read the story. Draw a picture in the last box to complete the story.

Marco likes to paint.   He likes to help his dad.

He is tired when he's finished.

Name _____

Predicting: Story Ending

Directions: Read each story. Circle the sentence that tells how the story will end.

Ann was riding her bike. She saw a dog in the park. She stopped to pet it. Ann left to go home.

The dog went swimming.

The dog followed Ann.

The dog went home with a cat.

Antonio went to a baseball game. A baseball player hit a ball toward him. He reached out his hands.

The player caught the ball.

The ball bounced on a car.

Antonio caught the ball.

Name _____

Making Inferences: Baseball

Traci likes baseball. She likes to win. Traci's team does not win.

Directions: Circle the correct answers.

1. Traci likes

football.   soccer.   baseball.

2. Traci likes to

win.

lose.

3. Traci uses a bat.

                    Yes   No

4. Traci is

happy.   sad.

Making Inferences: The Stars

Lynn looks at the stars. She sings a song about them. She makes a wish on them. The stars help Lynn sleep.

Directions: Circle the correct answers.

1. Lynn likes the

moon.

sun.

stars.

2. What song do you think she sings?

Row, Row, Row Your Boat

Twinkle, Twinkle Little Star

Happy Birthday to You

3. What does Lynn "make" on the stars?

a wish   a spaceship   lunch

Name _____

Making Inferences: Feelings

Directions: Read each story. Choose a word from the box to show how each person feels.

happy	excited	sad	mad

1. Andy and Sam were best friends. Sam and his family moved far away. How does Sam feel?

_____

- - - - - - - - - - - -

_____

2. Deana could not sleep. It was the night before her birthday party. How does Deana feel?

_____

- - - - - - - - - - - -

_____

3. Jacob let his baby brother play with his teddy bear. His brother lost the bear. How does Jacob feel?

_____

- - - - - - - - - - - -

_____

4. Kia picked flowers for her mom. Her mom smiled when she got them. How does Kia feel?

_____

- - - - - - - - - - - -

_____

Reading Comprehension

129

Total Basic Skills Grade 1

Books

Directions: What do you know about books? Use the words in the box below to help fill in the lines.

title	book	author
illustrator	pages	left to right
fun	library	glossary

The name of the book is the _____.

_____ is the direction we read.

The person who wrote the words is the _____.

Reading is _____ !

There are many books in the _____.

The person who draws the pictures is the _____.

The _____ is a kind of dictionary in the book to help you find the meanings of words.

Nouns

A noun is a word that names a person, place or thing. When you read a sentence, the noun is what the sentence is about.

Directions: Complete each sentence with a noun.

The _____ is fat.

My _____ is blue.

The _____ has apples.

The _____ is hot.

Nouns

Directions: Write these naming words in the correct box.

store	zoo	child	baby	teacher	table
cat	park	gym	woman	sock	horse

Person _____ _____

_____ _____

Place _____ _____

_____ _____

Thing _____ _____

_____ _____

Things That Go Together

Some nouns name things that go together.

Directions: Draw a line to match the nouns on the left with the things they go with on the right.

toothpaste

pencil

salt

shoe

soap

pillow

washcloth

sock

toothbrush

pepper

paper

bed

Name _____

Things That Go Together

Directions: Draw a line to connect the objects that go together.

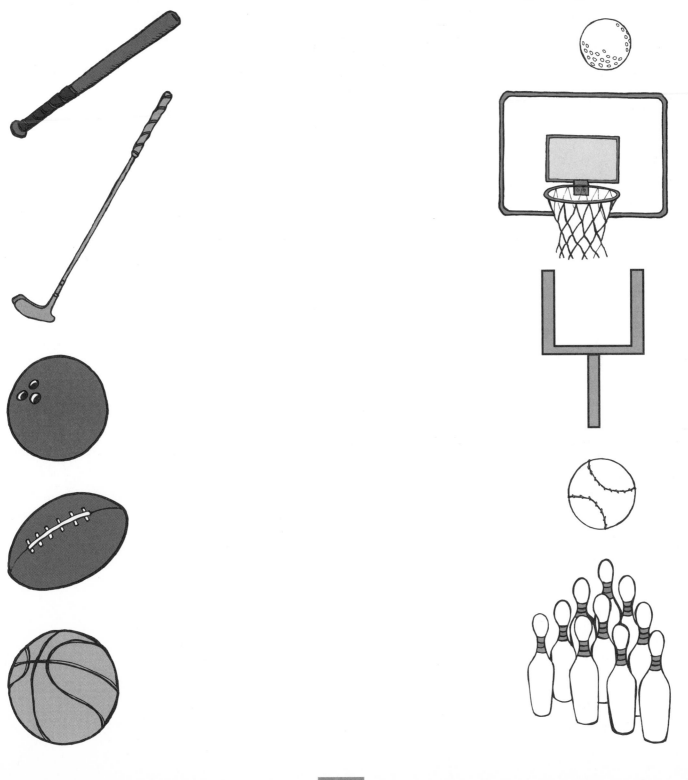

English

135

Total Basic Skills Grade 1

Verbs

Verbs are words that tell what a person or a thing can do.

Example: The girl pats the dog.

The word **pats** is the verb. It shows action.

Directions: Draw a line between the verbs and the pictures that show the action.

eat

run

sleep

swim

sing

hop

Verbs

Directions:
Look at the picture and read the words. Write an action word in each sentence below.

swing

rings

kick

run

talk

1. The two boys like to _____ together.

2. The children _____ the soccer ball.

3. Some children like to _____ on the swing.

4. The girl can _____ very fast.

5. The teacher _____ the bell.

Words That Describe

Describing words tell us more about a person, place or thing.

Directions: Read the words in the box. Choose the word that describes the picture. Write it next to the picture.

happy	round	sick	cold	long

Words That Describe

Directions: Read the words in the box. Choose the word that describes the picture. Write it next to the picture.

| wet | round | funny | soft | sad | tall |

Name _____

Words That Describe

Directions: Circle the describing word in each sentence. Draw a line from the sentence to the picture.

1. The hungry dog is eating.

2. The tiny bird is flying.

3. Horses have long legs.

4. She is a fast runner.

5. The little boy was lost.

Words That Describe: Colors and Numbers

Colors and numbers can describe nouns.

Directions: Underline the describing word in each sentence. Draw a picture to go with each sentence.

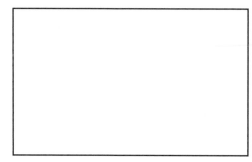

A yellow moon was in the sky.

Two worms are on the road.

The tree had red apples.

The girl wore a blue dress.

Sequencing: Comparative Adjectives

Directions: Look at each group of pictures. Write 1, 2 or 3 under the picture to show where it should be.

Example:

tallest __3__   **tall** __1__   **taller** __2__

small _____   **smallest** _____   **smaller** _____

biggest _____   **big** _____   **bigger** _____

wider _____   **wide** _____   **widest** _____

Sequencing: Comparative Adjectives

Directions: Look at the pictures in each row. Write 1, 2 or 3 under the picture to show where it should be.

shortest _____   shorter _____   short _____

longest _____   longer _____   long _____

happy _____   happier _____   happiest _____

hotter _____   hot _____   hottest _____

Synonyms

Synonyms are words that mean almost the same thing. **Start** and **begin** are synonyms.

Directions: Find the synonyms that describe each picture. Write the words in the boxes below the picture.

small   funny   large   sad   silly   little   big   unhappy

Similarities: Synonyms

Directions: Circle the word in each row that is most like the first word in the row.

Example:

grin   (smile)   frown   mad

bag   jar   sack   box

cat   fruit   animal   flower

apple   rot   cookie   fruit

around   circle   square   dot

brown   tan   black   red

bird   dog   cat   duck

bee   fish   ant   snake

Synonyms

Directions: Read each sentence and look at the underlined word. Circle the word that means the same thing. Write the new words.

1. The boy was <u>mad</u>.   happy   angry   pup

2. The <u>dog</u> is brown.   pup   cat   rat

3. I like to <u>scream</u>.   soar   mad   shout

4. The bird can <u>fly</u>.   soar   jog   warm

5. The girl can <u>run</u>.   sleep   jog   shout

6. I am <u>hot</u>.   warm   cold   soar

Name _____

Similarities: Synonyms

Directions: Read the story. Write a word on the line that means almost the same as the word under the line.

_____

- -

Dan went to the _____ .
 store

_____

- -

He wanted to buy _____ .
 food

_____

- -

He walked very _____ .
 quickly

The store had what he wanted. _____

- -

He bought it using _____ .
 dimes

_____

- -

Instead of walking home, Dan _____ .
 jogged

Antonyms

Antonyms are words that are opposites. **Hot** and **cold** are antonyms.
Directions: Draw a line between the antonyms.

closed

below

full

empty

above

old

new

open

Name _____

Opposites

Directions: Draw lines to connect the words that are opposites.

up	**wet**
over	**down**
dry	**dirty**
clean	**under**

Opposites

Opposites are things that are different in every way.

Directions: Draw a line between the opposites.

day

happy

big

open

front

little

closed

night

back

sad

Opposites

Directions: Circle the picture in each row that is the opposite of the first picture.

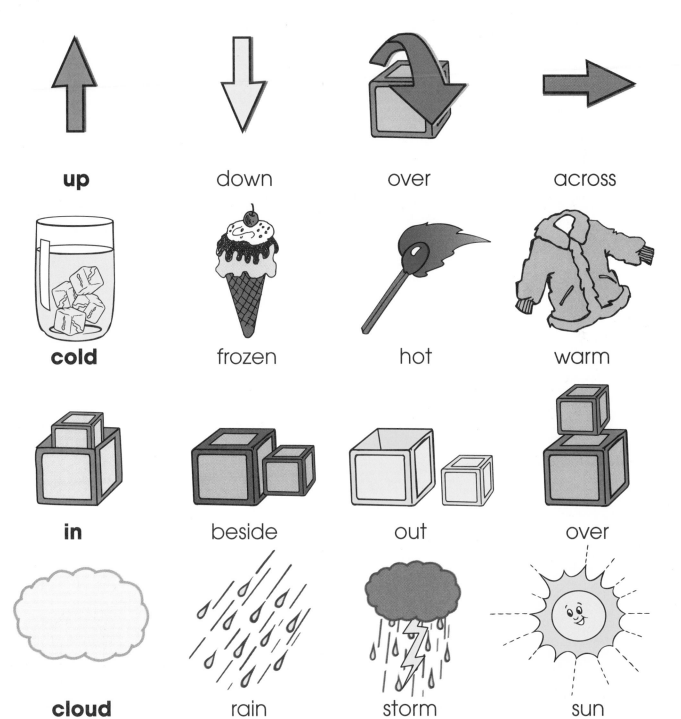

up   down   over   across

cold   frozen   hot   warm

in   beside   out   over

cloud   rain   storm   sun

Opposites

Directions: Read each clue. Write the answers in the puzzle.

high   yes   left
heavy   tight
safe   full

Across:

1. Opposite of low
2. Opposite of no
4. Opposite of empty
6. Opposite of loose

Down:

1. Opposite of light
3. Opposite of dangerous
5. Opposite of right

Name _____

Homophones

Homophones are words that **sound** the same but are spelled differently and mean something different. **Blew** and **blue** are homophones.

Directions: Look at the word pairs. Choose the word that describes the picture. Write the word on the line next to the picture.

1. sew   so

_____

2. pair   pear

_____

3. eye   I

_____

4. see   sea

_____

Name _____

Homophones

Directions: Read each sentence. Underline the two words that sound the same but are spelled differently and mean something different.

1. Tom ate eight grapes.

2. Becky read *Little Red Riding Hood*.

3. I went to buy two dolls.

4. Five blue feathers blew in the wind.

5. Would you get wood for the fire?

Name _____

Sentences

Sentences begin with capital letters.

Directions: Read the sentences and write them below. Begin each sentence with a capital letter.

Example: the cat is fat.

The cat is fat.

my dog is big.

_____

the boy is sad.

_____

bikes are fun!

_____

dad can bake.

_____

English   155   Total Basic Skills Grade 1

Name _____

Word Order

If you change the order of the words in a sentence, you can change the meaning of the sentence.

Directions: Read the sentences. Draw a circle around the sentence that describes the picture.

Example:

(The fox jumped over the dogs.)
The dogs jumped over the fox.

1. The cat watched the bird.
   The bird watched the cat.

2. The girl looked at the boy.
   The boy looked at the girl.

3. The turtle ran past the rabbit.
   The rabbit ran past the turtle.

Word Order

Directions: Look at the picture. Put the words in order. Write the sentences on the lines below.

1. We made lemonade. some
2. good. It was
3. We the sold lemonade.
4. cost It five cents.
5. fun. We had

1. _____

2. _____

3. _____

4. _____

5. _____

Telling Sentences

Directions: Read the sentences and write them below. Begin each sentence with a capital letter. End each sentence with a period.

1. most children like pets
2. some children like dogs
3. some children like cats
4. some children like snakes
5. some children like all animals

1. _____

2. _____

3. _____

4. _____

5. _____

Telling Sentences

Directions: Read the sentences and write them below.
Begin each sentence with a capital letter.
End each sentence with a period.

1. i like to go to the store with Mom
2. we go on Friday
3. i get to push the cart
4. i get to buy the cookies
5. i like to help Mom

1. _____

2. _____

3. _____

4. _____

5. _____

Asking Sentences

Directions: Write the first word of each asking sentence. Be sure to begin each question with a capital letter. End each question with a question mark.

1. _____ you like the zoo   **do**

2. _____ much does it cost   **how**

3. _____ you feed the ducks   **can**

4. _____ you see the monkeys   **will**

5. _____ time will you eat lunch   **what**

Asking Sentences

Directions: Read the asking sentences. Write the sentences below. Begin each sentence with a capital letter. End each sentence with a question mark.

1. what game will we play
2. do you like to read
3. how old are you
4. who is your best friend
5. can you tie your shoes

1. _____

2. _____

3. _____

4. _____

5. _____

GRADE 1

Name _____

Periods and Question Marks

Directions: Put a period or a question mark at the end of each sentence below.

1. Do you like parades

2. The clowns lead the parade

3. Can you hear the band

4. The balloons are big

5. Can you see the horses

Name _____

Is and Are

We use **is** in sentences about one person or one thing. We use **are** in sentences about more than one person or thing.

Example: The dog **is** barking.
The dogs **are** barking.

Directions: Write **is** or **are** in the sentences below.

1. Jim _____ playing baseball.

2. Fred and Sam _____ good friends.

3. Cupcakes _____ my favorite treat.

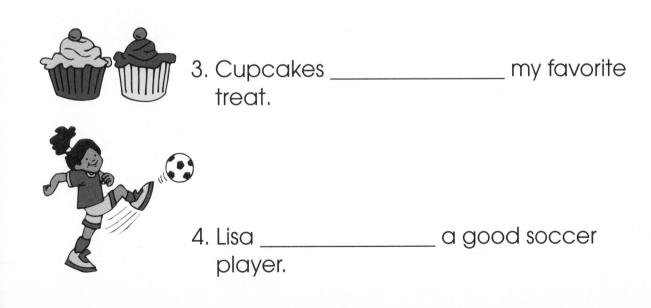

4. Lisa _____ a good soccer player.

Is and Are

Directions: Write **is** or **are** in the sentences below.

Example: Lisa __is__ sleeping.

1. Cats and dogs _____ good pets.

2. Bill _____ my best friend.

3. Apples _____ good to eat.

4. We _____ going to the zoo.

5. Pedro _____ coming to my house.

6. When _____ you all going to the zoo?

Name _____

Color Names

Directions: Trace the letters to write the name of each color. Then write the name again by yourself.

Example:

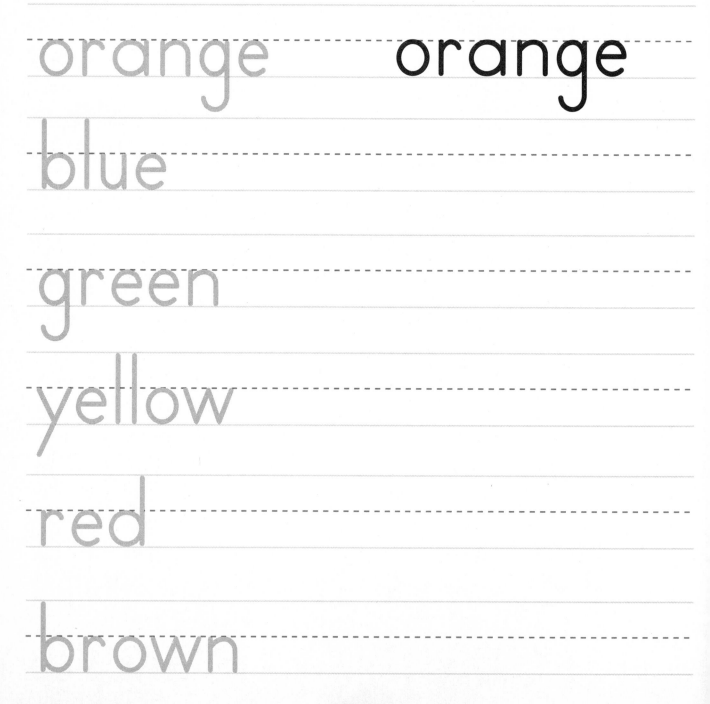

orange   orange

blue

green

yellow

red

brown

Color Names: Sentences

Directions: Use the color words to complete these sentences. Then put a period at the end.

Example: My new 🧤 are **orange.**

| green tree | blue bike | yellow chick | red ball |

1. The baby 🐤 is _____ ☐

2. This 🌳 is _____ ☐

3. My 🔴 is big and _____ ☐

4. My sister's 🚲 is _____ ☐

Name _____

Animal Names

Directions: Fill in the missing letters for each word.

Example:

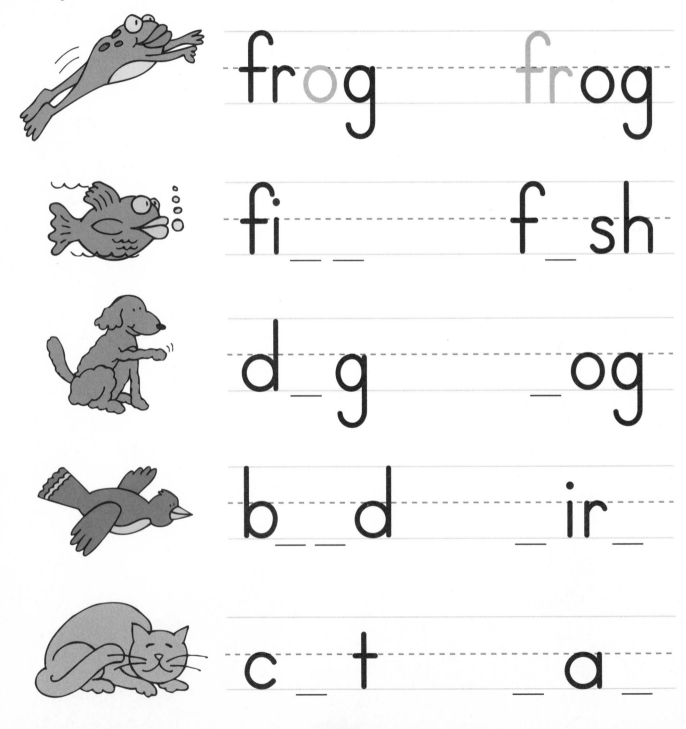

frog   frog

fi _ _   f _ sh

d _ g   _ og

b _ d   _ ir _

c _ t   _ a _

Animal Names: Sentences

A **sentence** tells about something.

Directions: These sentences tell about animals. Write the word that completes each sentence.

Example:

My *frog* jumps high.

1. I take my _____ for a walk.

2. My _____ lives in water.

3. My _____ can sing.

4. My _____ has a long tail.

Name _____

Things That Go

Directions: Trace the letters to write the name of each thing. Write each name again by yourself. Then color the pictures.

Example:

car   car

truck

train

bike

plane

Things That Go: Sentences

Directions: These sentences tell about things that go. Write the word that completes each sentence.

Example:

The **car** is in the garage.

1. The _____ was at the farm.

2. My _____ had a flat tire.

3. The _____ flew high.

4. The _____ went fast.

Name _____

Clothing Words

Directions: Trace the letters to write the name of each clothing word. Then write each name again by yourself.

Example:

shirt   shirt

pants

jacket

socks

shoes

dress

hat

Name _____

Clothing Words: Sentences

Directions: Some of these sentences tell a whole idea. Others have something missing. If something is missing, draw a line to the word that completes the sentence. Put a period at the end of each sentence.

Example:

She is wearing a polka-dot

holes

1. The baseball player wore a

2. His pants were torn.

dress .

3. The socks had

4. The jacket had blue buttons.

hat

5. The shoes were brown.

GRADE 1

Name _____

Food Names

Directions: Trace the letters to write the name of each food word. Write each name again by yourself. Then color the pictures.

Example:

bread **bread**

cookie

apple

cake

milk

egg

Name _____

Food Names: Asking Sentences

An **asking sentence** asks a question. Asking sentences end with a question mark.

Directions: Write each sentence on the line. Begin each sentence with a capital letter. Put a period at the end of the telling sentences and a question mark at the end of the asking sentences.

Example: do you like cake

Do you like cake?

1. the cow has spots

2. is that cookie good

3. she ate the apple

Name _____

Number Words

Directions: Trace the letters to write the name of each number. Write the numbers again by yourself. Then color the number pictures.

Example:

1 one **one**

2 two

3 three

4 four

5 five

6 six

7 seven

8 eight

9 nine

10 ten

Name _____

Number Words: Asking Sentences

Directions: Use a number word to answer each question.

one	five	seven	three	eight

1. How many trees are there?

2. How many flowers are there?

3. How many presents are there?

4. How many clocks are there?

5. How many forks are there?

Spelling

177

Total Basic Skills Grade 1

Action Words

Action words tell things we can do.

Directions: Trace the letters to write each action word. Then write the action word again by yourself.

Example:

sleep   sleep

run

make

ride

play

stop

Name _____

Action Words: More Than One

To show more than one of something, add **s** to the end of the word.

Example: one cat   two cats

Directions: In each sentence, add **s** to show more than one. Then write the action word that completes each sentence.

sit	jump	stop	ride

Example:

The frog **s** **sleep** in the sun.

1. The boy _____ _____ on the fence.

2. The car _____ _____ at the sign.

3. The girl _____ _____ in the water.

4. The dog _____ _____ in the wagon.

Spelling

Total Basic Skills Grade 1

Action Words: Asking Sentences

Directions: Write an asking sentence about each picture. Begin each sentence with **can**. Add an action word. Begin each asking sentence with a capital letter and end it with a question mark.

Example:

I with you can

Can I sit with you?

she can

_____

with you can I

_____

can she fast

_____

Name _____

Sense Words

Directions: Circle the word that is spelled correctly. Then write the correct spelling in the blank.

Example:

tast
(taste)
tste

taste

touch
tuch
touh

smel
smll
smell

her
hear
har

see
se
sea

Name _____

Sense Words: Sentences

Directions: Read each sentence and write the correct words in the blanks.

Example:

taste
mouth   I can **taste** things with my **mouth**.

touch
hands   1. I can _____ things with my _____.

nose
smell   2. I can _____ things with my _____.

hear
ears   3. I can _____ with my _____.

see
eyes   4. I can _____ things with my _____.

Total Basic Skills Grade 1   182   Spelling

Weather Words: Beginning Sounds

Directions: Say the sound of the letter at the beginning of each row. Find the pictures in each row that begin with the same letter. Write the letter under the pictures.

Example:

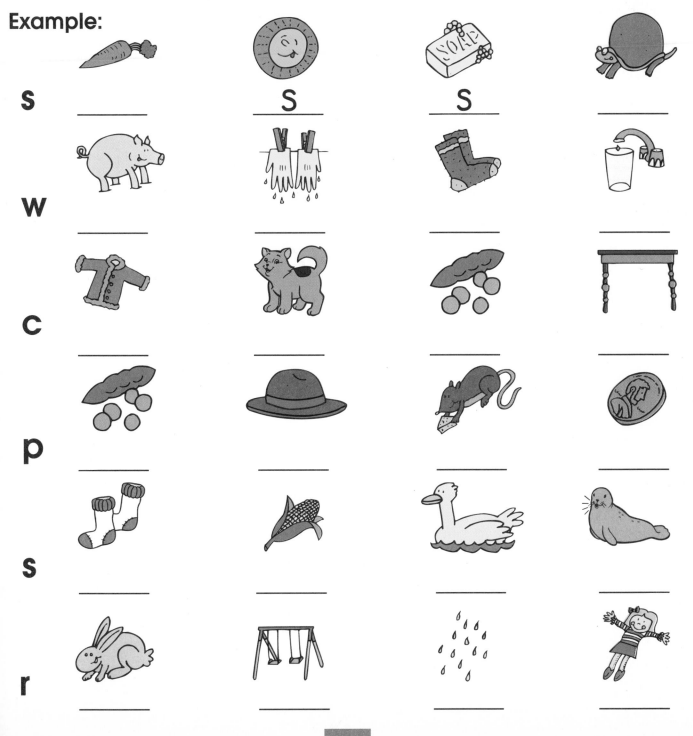

s ____	S	S	____
w ____	____	____	____
c ____	____	____	____
p ____	____	____	____
s ____	____	____	____
r ____	____	____	____

Weather Words: Sentences

Directions: Write the weather word that completes each sentence. Put a period at the end of the telling sentences and a question mark at the end of the asking sentences.

Example:

Do flowers grow in the ___ sun ? .

| rain | water | wet | hot |

1. The sun makes me _____ ☐

2. When it rains, the grass gets _____ ☐

3. Do you think it will _____ on our picnic ☐

4. Should you drink the _____ from the rain ☐

My World

Directions: Fill in the missing letters for each word.

tree

gr__ss

fl_____er

p_nd

s__nd

sk__

tree

____ __a____

__ ____ow____

_____o

__ __a__ ____

_____ ____y

Name _____

My World

Directions: The letters in the words below are mixed up. Unscramble the letters and write each word correctly.

etre _____

srags _____

loefwr _____

dnop _____

dnsa _____

yks _____

Name _____

My World: Sentences

Directions: Write the word that completes each sentence. Put a period at the end of the telling sentences and a question mark at the end of the asking sentences.

Example: Does the sun shine on the $\underline{\text{flowers}}$?

tree	grass	pond	sand	sky

1. The _____ was full of dark clouds☐

2. Can you climb the _____ ☐

3. Did you see the duck in the _____ ☐

4. Is the child playing in the _____ ☐

5. The _____ in the yard was tall☐

The Parts of My Body: Sentences

Directions: Write the word that completes each sentence. Put a period at the end of the telling sentences and a question mark at the end of the asking sentences.

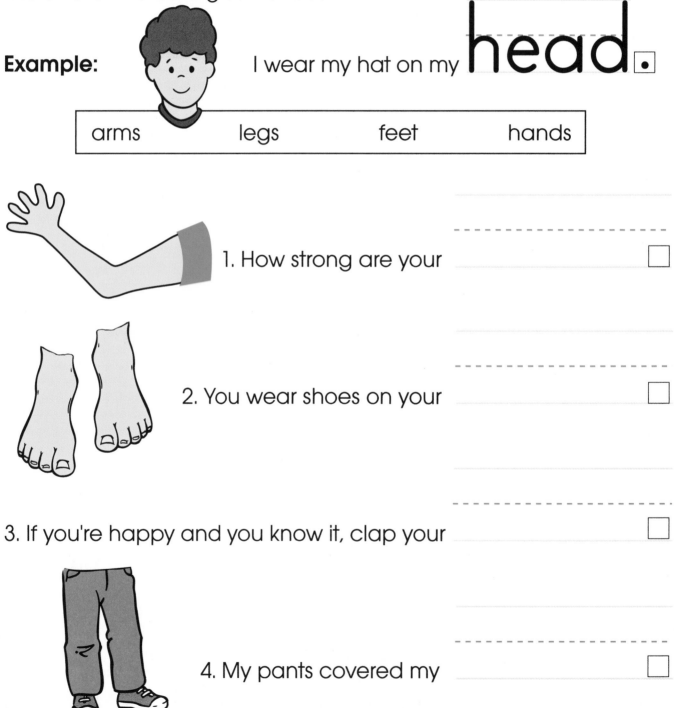

Example: I wear my hat on my **head**.

| arms | legs | feet | hands |

1. How strong are your ☐

2. You wear shoes on your ☐

3. If you're happy and you know it, clap your ☐

4. My pants covered my ☐

The Parts of My Body: Sentences

Directions: Read the sentence parts below. Draw a line from the first part of the sentence to the second part that completes it.

1. I give big hugs

    with my arms.

    with my car.

2. My feet

    drive the car.

    got wet in the rain.

3. I have a bump

    on my head.

    on my coat.

4. My mittens

    keep my arms warm.

    keep my hands warm.

5. I can jump high

    using my legs.

    using a spoon.

Name _____

The Parts of My Body: Sentences

Directions: Read the two sentences on each line and draw a line between them. Then write each sentence again on the lines below. Begin each sentence with a capital letter, and end each one with a period or a question mark.

Example: wash your hands|they are dirty

Wash your hands.
They are dirty.

1. you have big arms are you very strong

_ _

_ _

_ _

2. I have two feet I can run fast

_ _

_ _

_ _

Number Recognition

Directions: Write the numbers 1-10. Color the bear.

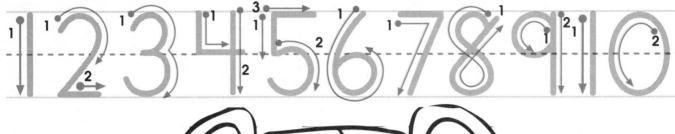

Number Recognition

Directions: Count the number of objects in each group. Draw a line to the correct number.

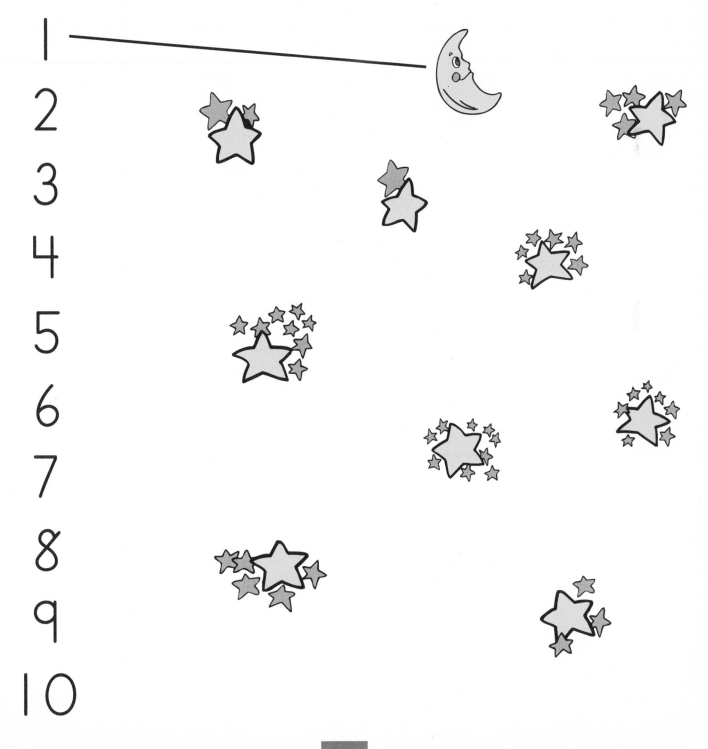

1
2
3
4
5
6
7
8
9
10

Name _____

Counting

Directions: How many are there of each shape? Write the answers in the boxes. The first one is done for you.

GRADE 1

Name _____

Counting

Directions: How many are there of each picture? Write the answers in the boxes. The first one is done for you.

Name _____

Number Word Find

Directions: Find the number words 0 through 12 hidden in the box.

```
t e a z w z x a b i g t e n
o l z r b e r e v e d l a j
t w e l v e a b o n e c d z
i a r p q d p s u j x e i w
c f o p l s c k i q u i i o
m s t f v i o e t t f g h d
t n u w u x g z w h g h r o
n i n e k f d f o u r t j f
a s g l q c w k o s n v m i
n y c e b o n h h p o m p v
b e x v s s e v e n w e n e
t h r e e r t a l j k x q z
m o a n e n i m u t w a y x
```

Words to find:

zero four eight eleven
one five nine twelve
two six ten
three seven

Number Words

Directions: Number the buildings from one to six.

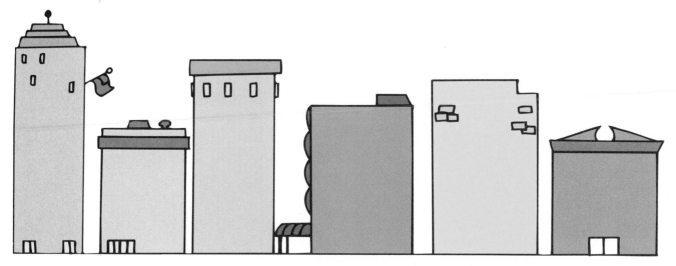

Directions: Draw a line from the word to the number.

two	1
five	3
six	5
four	6
one	2
three	4

Name _____

Number Words

Directions: Number the buildings from five to ten.

Directions: Draw a line from the word to the number.

nine	8
seven	10
five	7
eight	5
six	9
ten	6

Name _____

Number Recognition Review

Directions: Match the correct number of objects with the number. Then match the number with the word.

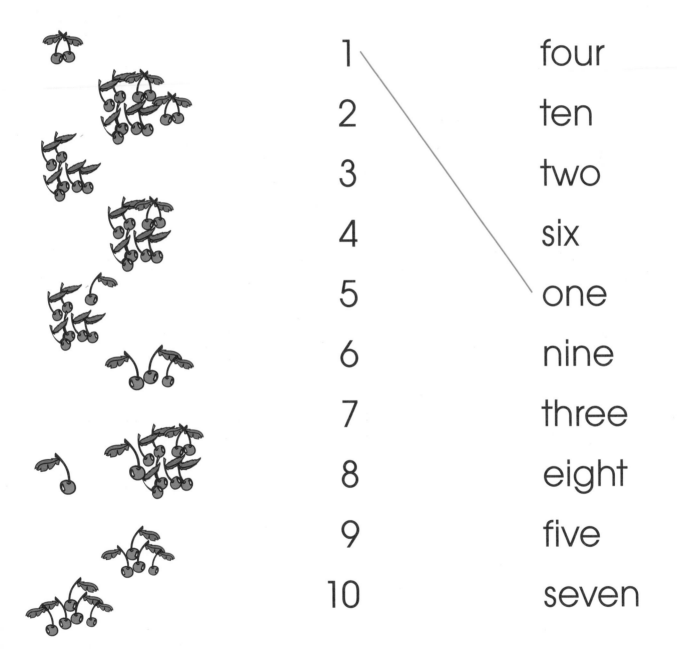

1		four
2		ten
3		two
4		six
5		one
6		nine
7		three
8		eight
9		five
10		seven

Sequencing Numbers

Sequencing is putting numbers in the correct order.

1, 2, 3, 4, 5, 6, 7, 8, 9, 10

Directions: Write the missing numbers.

Example: 4, _____5_____ ,6

3, _____ ,5   7, _____ ,9   8, _____ ,10

6, _____ ,8   _____ ,3 ,4   _____ ,5 ,6

5, 6, _____   _____ ,6 ,7   _____ ,3 ,4

_____ ,4 ,5   _____ ,7 ,8   5, _____ ,7

2, 3, _____   1, 2, _____   7, 8, _____

2, _____ ,4   _____ ,2 ,3   4, _____ ,6

6, 7, _____   3, 4, _____   1, _____ ,3

7, 8, _____   _____ ,3 ,4   _____ ,9 ,10

Name _____

Number Match

Directions: Cut out the pictures and number words below. Mix them up and match them again.

one		two	eight
		five	
	three		nine
four		seven	
	six		ten

Page is blank for cutting exercise on previous page.

Name _____

Number Crossword Puzzle

Directions: Write the correct number word in the boxes provided.

Across
2. 4
3. 8
5. 2
7. 7
9. 10

Down
1. 0
2. 5
4. 3
6. 1
7. 6
8. 9

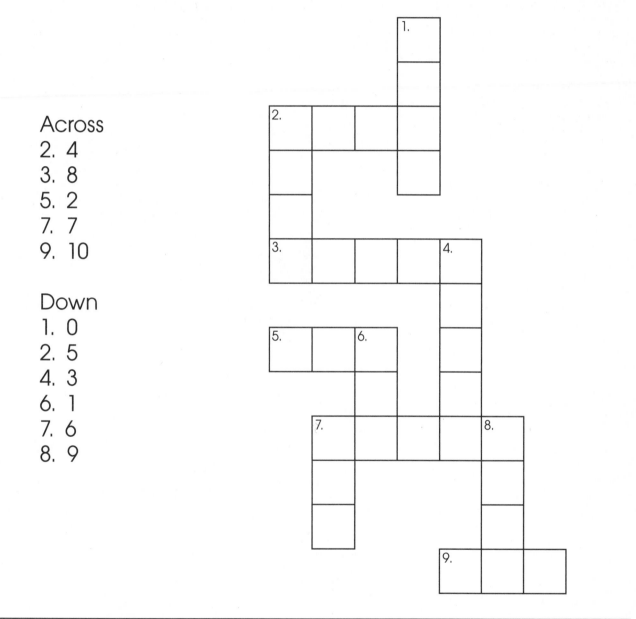

one	two	three	four	five
●	●●	●●●	●●●●	●●●●●

six	seven	eight	nine	ten	zero
●●● ●●●	●●●● ●●●	●●●● ●●●●	●●●●● ●●●●	●●●●● ●●●●●	

Ordinal Numbers

Ordinal numbers are used to indicate order in a series, such as **first**, **second** or **third**.

Directions: Draw a line to the picture that corresponds to the ordinal number in the left column.

eighth

third

sixth

ninth

seventh

second

fourth

first

fifth

tenth

Ordinal Numbers

Directions: Draw an **X** on the first vegetable, draw a circle around the second vegetable, and draw a square around the third vegetable.

Directions: Write the ordinal number below the picture.

✂ **Cut** the children apart. Mix them up. Then put them back in the correct order.

| first | second | third | fourth | fifth | sixth | seventh | eighth | ninth | tenth |

Page is blank for cutting exercise on previous page.

Sequencing: At the Movies

Directions: The children are watching a movie. Read the sentences. Cut out the pictures below. Glue them where they belong in the picture.

1. The first child is eating popcorn.
2. The third child is eating candy.
3. The fourth child has a cup of fruit punch.
4. The second child is eating a big pretzel.

Page is blank for cutting exercise on previous page.

Name _____

Sequencing: Standing in Line

Directions: These children are waiting to see a movie. Look at them and follow the instructions.

1. Color the person who is first in line yellow.

2. Color the person who is last in line brown.

3. Color the person who is second in line pink.

4. Circle the person who is at the end of the line.

Addition 1, 2

Addition means "putting together" or adding two or more numbers to find the sum. "+" is a plus sign. It means to add the 2 numbers. "=" is an equals sign. It tells how much they are together.

Directions: Count the cats and tell how many.

Name _____

Addition

Directions: Count the shapes and write the numbers below to tell how many in all.

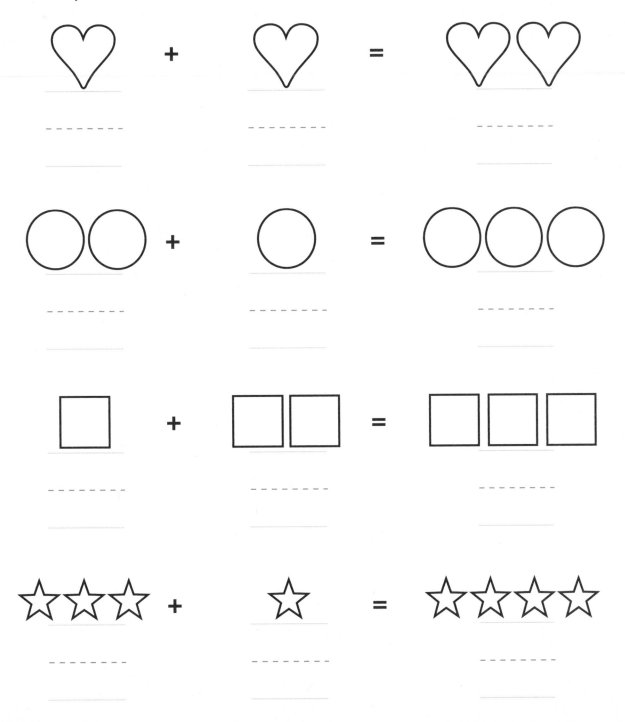

Name _____

Addition

Directions: Draw the correct number of dots next to the numbers in each problem. Add up the number of dots to find your answer.

Example:

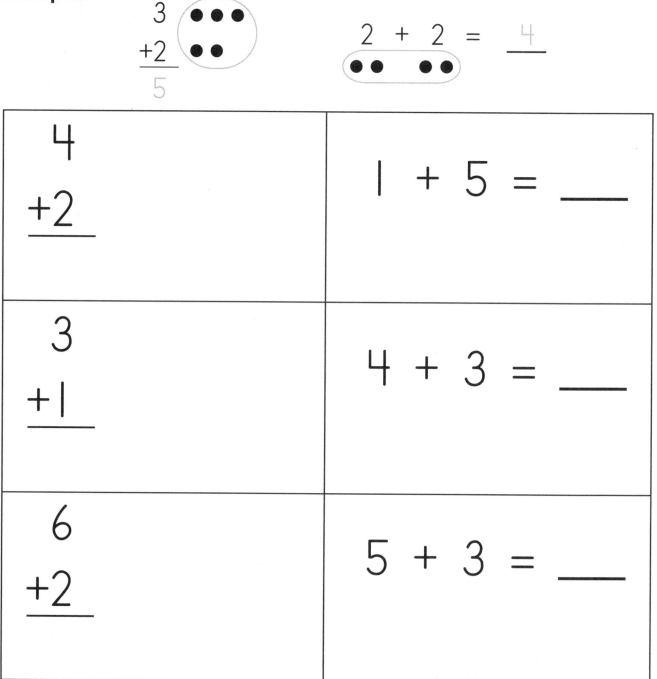

$$3$$
$$+2$$
$$\overline{5}$$

$$2 + 2 = \underline{4}$$

$$4$$
$$+2$$

$$1 + 5 = \underline{\ \ }$$

$$3$$
$$+1$$

$$4 + 3 = \underline{\ \ }$$

$$6$$
$$+2$$

$$5 + 3 = \underline{\ \ }$$

Addition 3, 4, 5, 6

Directions: Practice writing the numbers and then add. Draw dots to help, if needed.

3

4

5

6

$$\begin{array}{r} 2 \\ +4 \\ \hline \end{array} \qquad \begin{array}{r} 1 \\ +4 \\ \hline \end{array}$$

$$\begin{array}{r} 3 \\ +2 \\ \hline \end{array} \qquad \begin{array}{r} 1 \\ +2 \\ \hline \end{array}$$

Name _____

Addition 4, 5, 6, 7

Directions: Practice writing the numbers and then add. Draw dots to help, if needed.

4 - - - - - - - - - - - - - - - - - - -

$$\begin{array}{r} 2 \\ +5 \\ \hline \end{array}$$ $$\begin{array}{r} 3 \\ +1 \\ \hline \end{array}$$

5 - - - - - - - - - - - - - - - - - - -

6 - - - - - - - - - - - - - - - - - - -

7 - - - - - - - - - - - - - - - - - - -

$$\begin{array}{r} 4 \\ +1 \\ \hline \end{array}$$ $$\begin{array}{r} 2 \\ +4 \\ \hline \end{array}$$

Name _____

Addition 6, 7, 8

Directions: Practice writing the numbers and then add. Draw dots to help, if needed.

6 - - - - - - - - - - - - - - -

7 - - - - - - - - - - - - - - -

8 - - - - - - - - - - - - - - -

$$\begin{array}{r}3\\+4\\\hline\end{array}$$

$$\begin{array}{r}5\\+1\\\hline\end{array}$$

$$\begin{array}{r}2\\+6\\\hline\end{array}$$

$$\begin{array}{r}4\\+4\\\hline\end{array}$$

Math

215

Total Basic Skills Grade 1

Name _____

Addition 7, 8, 9

Directions: Practice writing the numbers and then add. Draw dots to help, if needed.

7

8

9

$$8 + 1$$

$$3 + 5$$

$$2 + 7$$

$$6 + 1$$

Name _____

Addition Table

Directions: Add across and down with a friend. Fill in the spaces.

+	0	1	2	3	4	5
0	0					
1	1	2				
2			4			
3	3			6		
4						
5						10

Do you notice any number patterns in the Addition Table?

Name _____

Subtraction 1, 2, 3

Subtraction means "taking away" or subtracting one number from another. "–" is a minus sign. It means to subtract the second number from the first.

Directions: Practice writing the numbers and then subtract. Draw dots and cross them out, if needed.

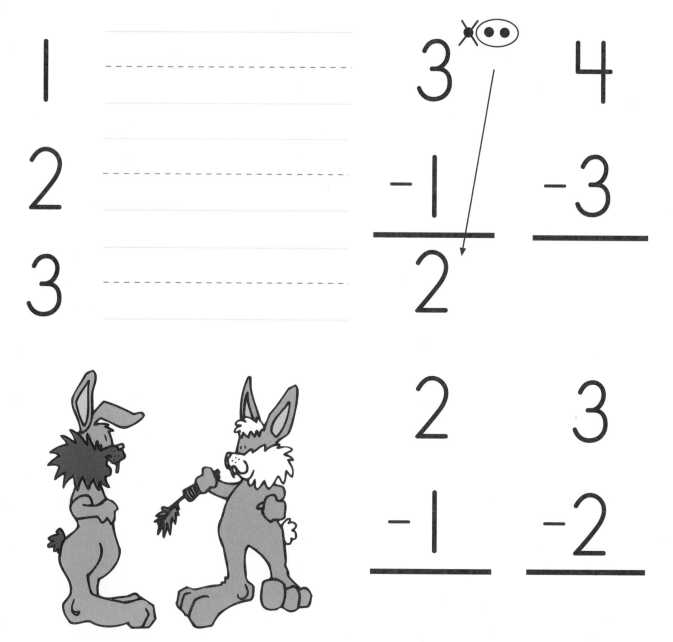

$$1$$

$$2$$

$$3$$

$$\begin{array}{r} 3 \\ -1 \\ \hline 2 \end{array}$$

$$\begin{array}{r} 4 \\ -3 \\ \hline \end{array}$$

$$\begin{array}{r} 2 \\ -1 \\ \hline \end{array}$$

$$\begin{array}{r} 3 \\ -2 \\ \hline \end{array}$$

ServeName _____

Subtraction 3, 4, 5, 6

Directions: Practice writing the numbers and then subtract.
Draw dots and cross them out, if needed.

3   5   6
          -2   -1
4   ____   ____

5

6   6   5
          -3   -1
          ____   ____

Name _____

Subtraction

Directions: Draw the correct number of dots next to the numbers in each problem. Cross out the ones subtracted to find your answer.

Example:

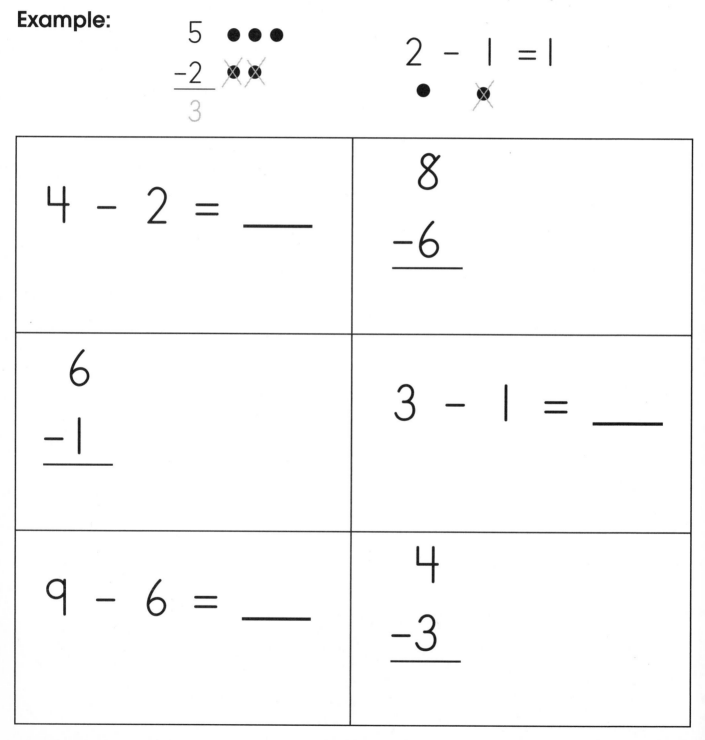

Name _____

Review

Directions: Trace the numbers. Work the problems.

1 2 3 4 5 6 7 8 9 10

q
-3
___

6
+2
___

3
+4
___

2
-1
___

5
+4
___

q
-5
___

7
+2
___

8
-6
___

4
-2
___

6
+3
___

q
-7
___

1
+7
___

Zero

Directions: Write the number.

Example:

How many monkeys?

3

How many monkeys?

0

How many
kites?

How many
kites?

How many flowers?

How many flowers?

How many apples?

How many apples?

Name _____

Zero

Directions: Write the number that tells how many.

How many sailboats?

- - - - - - - - - - - -

How many sailboats?

- - - - - - - - - - - -

How many eggs?

- - - - - - - - - - - -

How many eggs?

- - - - - - - - - - - -

How many marshmallows?

- - - - - - - - - - - -

How many marshmallows?

- - - - - - - - - - - -

How many candles?

- - - - - - - - - - - -

How many candles?

- - - - - - - - - - - -

Picture Problems: Addition

Directions: Solve the number problem under each picture.

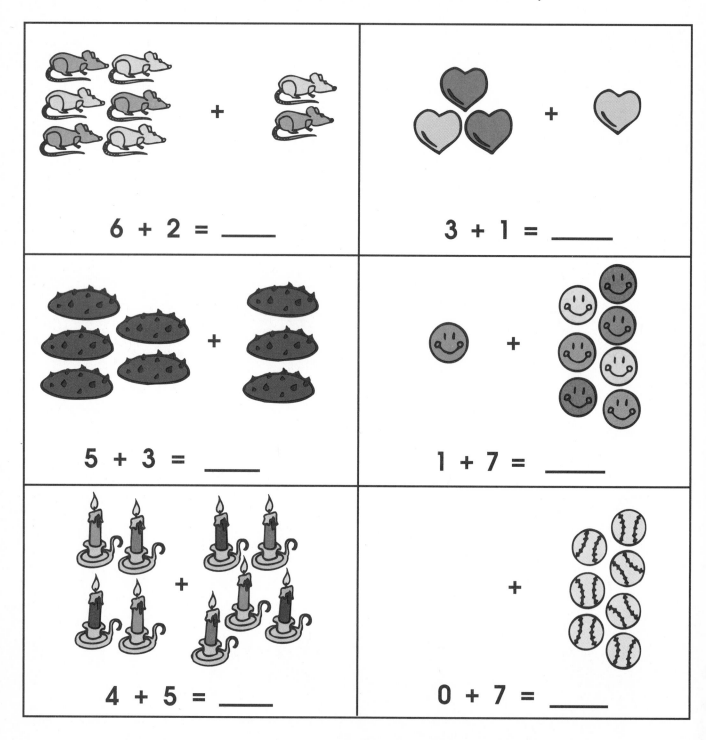

6 + 2 = _____

3 + 1 = _____

5 + 3 = _____

1 + 7 = _____

4 + 5 = _____

0 + 7 = _____

Name _____

Picture Problems: Addition

Directions: Solve the number problem under each picture.

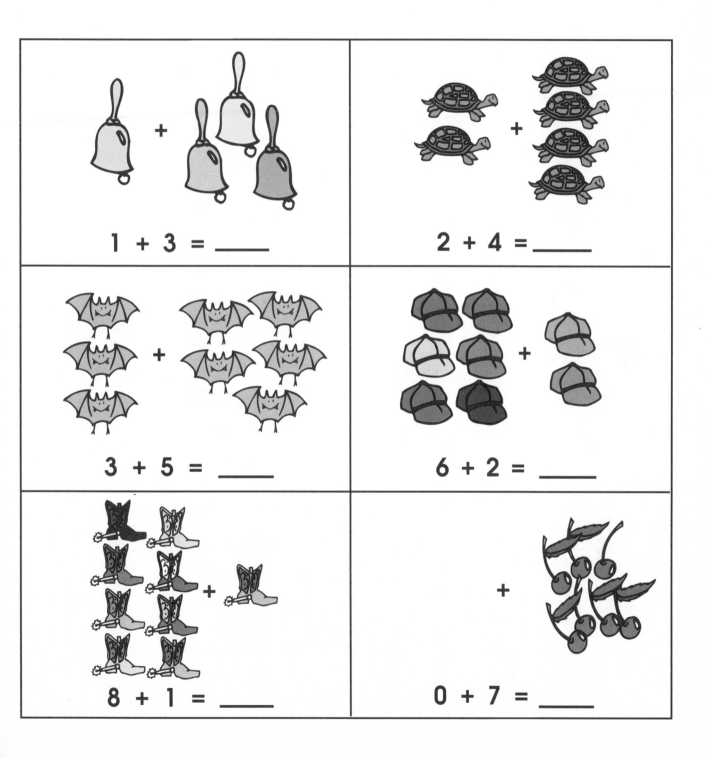

1 + 3 = ____

2 + 4 = ____

3 + 5 = ____

6 + 2 = ____

8 + 1 = ____

0 + 7 = ____

Name _____

Picture Problems: Subtraction

Directions: Solve the number problem under each picture.

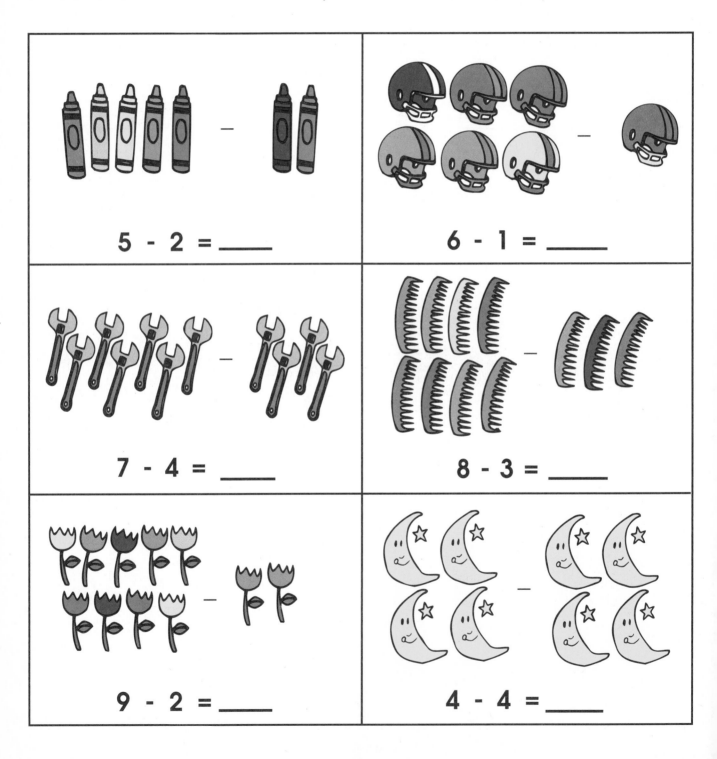

5 - 2 = _____

6 - 1 = _____

7 - 4 = _____

8 - 3 = _____

9 - 2 = _____

4 - 4 = _____

Name _____

Picture Problems: Subtraction

Directions: Solve the number problem under each picture.

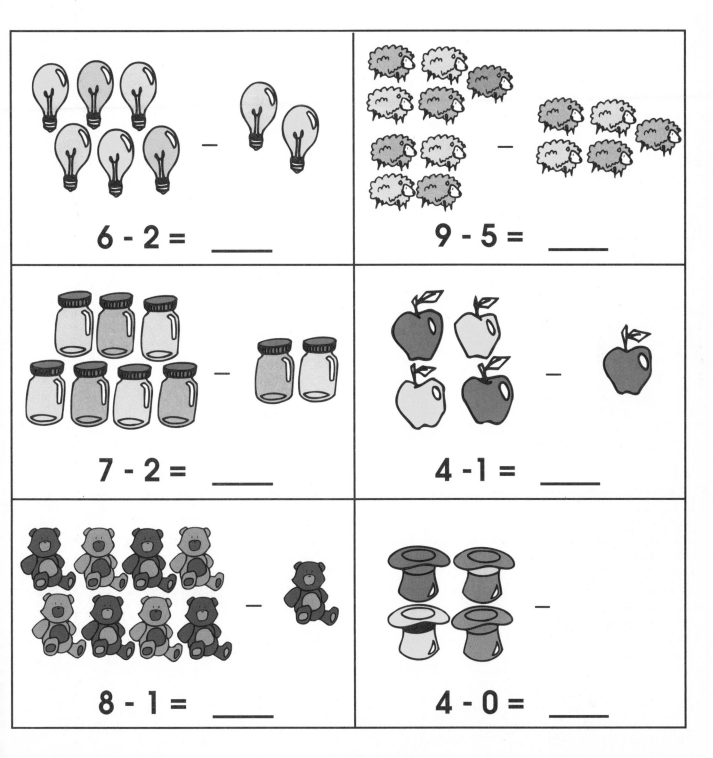

6 - 2 = _____

9 - 5 = _____

7 - 2 = _____

4 - 1 = _____

8 - 1 = _____

4 - 0 = _____

Math

227

Total Basic Skills Grade 1

Name _____

Picture Problems: Addition and Subtraction

Directions: Solve the number problem under each picture.

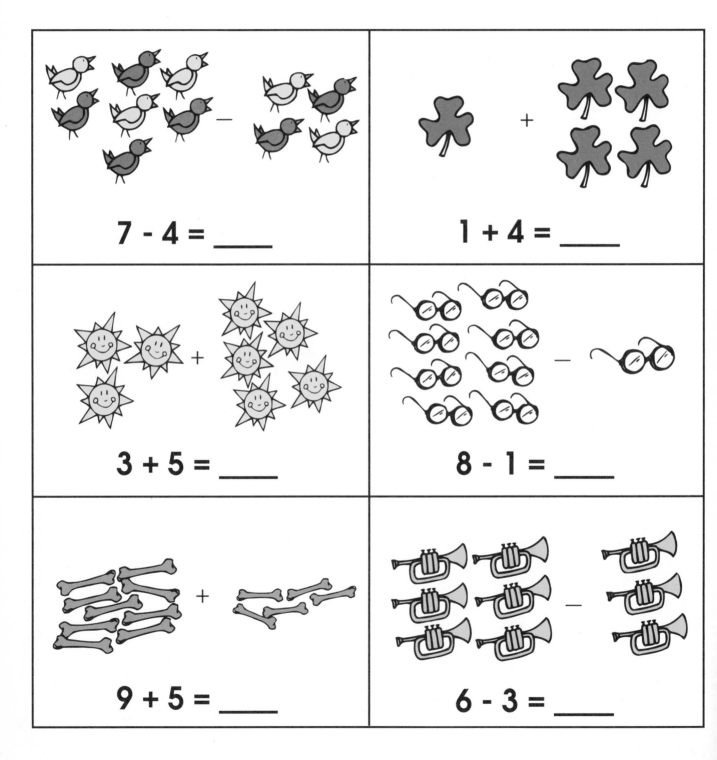

7 - 4 = _____

1 + 4 = _____

3 + 5 = _____

8 - 1 = _____

9 + 5 = _____

6 - 3 = _____

Name _____

Picture Problems: Addition and Subtraction

Directions: Solve the number problem under each picture.
Write **+** or **–** to show if you should add or subtract.

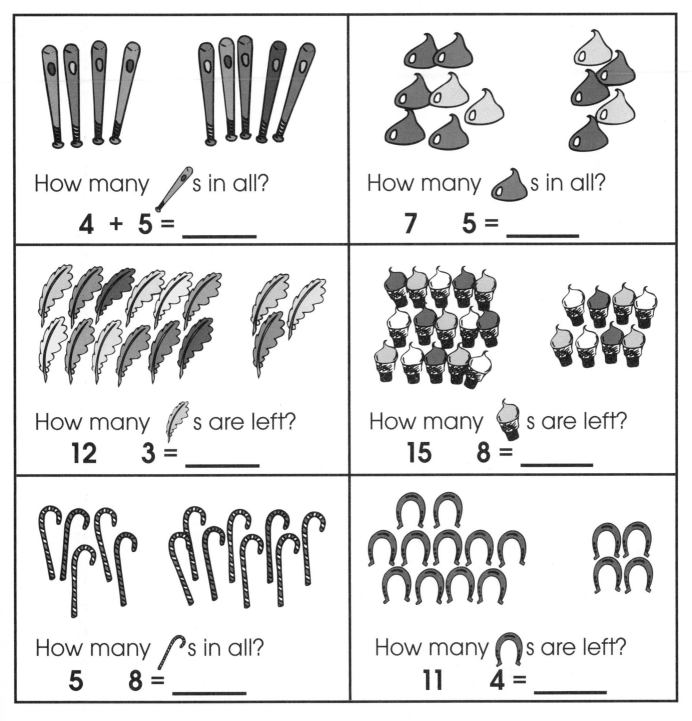

How many s in all?

4 + 5 = _____

How many s in all?

7 _ 5 = _____

How many s are left?

12 _ 3 = _____

How many s are left?

15 _ 8 = _____

How many s in all?

5 _ 8 = _____

How many s are left?

11 _ 4 = _____

Name _____

Picture Problems: Addition and Subtraction

Directions: Solve the number problem under each picture.
Write **+** or **−** to show if you should add or subtract.

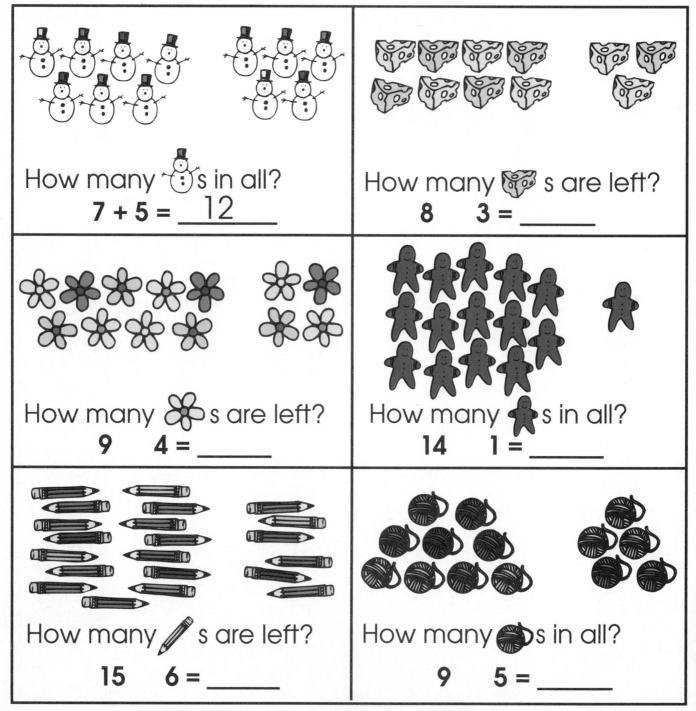

How many 👻s in all?

7 + 5 = ___12___

How many 🧀 s are left?

8 ___ 3 = _____

How many 🌸s are left?

9 ___ 4 = _____

How many 🍪s in all?

14 ___ 1 = _____

How many ✏️s are left?

15 ___ 6 = _____

How many 🧶s in all?

9 ___ 5 = _____

GRADE 1

Name _____

Review: Addition and Subtraction

Directions: Solve the number problem under each picture.
Write **+** or **−** to show if you should add or subtract.

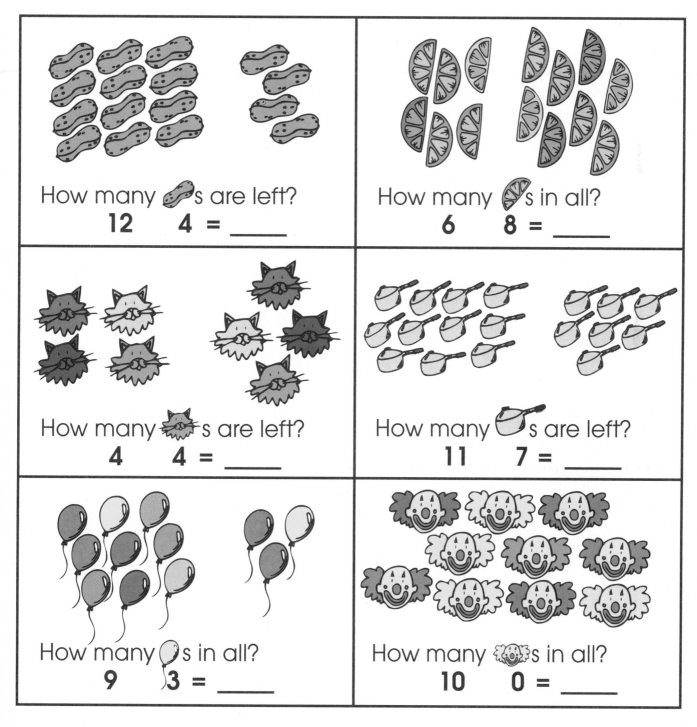

How many 🥜s are left?

12 ___ **4** = ____

How many 🍊s in all?

6 ___ **8** = ____

How many 🐱s are left?

4 ___ **4** = ____

How many 🍳s are left?

11 ___ **7** = ____

How many 🎈s in all?

9 ___ **3** = ____

How many 🤡s in all?

10 ___ **0** = ____

Name _____

Addition 1-5

Directions: Count the tools in each tool box. Write your answers in the blanks. Circle the problem that matches your answer.

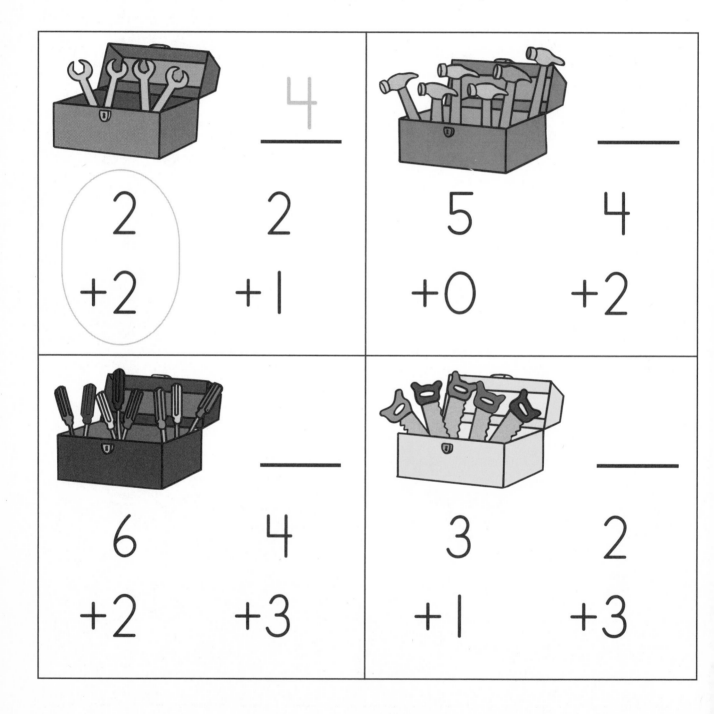

$$\underline{4}$$

$$\begin{array}{r} 2 \\ +2 \\ \hline \end{array}$$ $$\begin{array}{r} 2 \\ +1 \\ \hline \end{array}$$

$$\underline{}$$

$$\begin{array}{r} 5 \\ +0 \\ \hline \end{array}$$ $$\begin{array}{r} 4 \\ +2 \\ \hline \end{array}$$

$$\underline{}$$

$$\begin{array}{r} 6 \\ +2 \\ \hline \end{array}$$ $$\begin{array}{r} 4 \\ +3 \\ \hline \end{array}$$

$$\underline{}$$

$$\begin{array}{r} 3 \\ +1 \\ \hline \end{array}$$ $$\begin{array}{r} 2 \\ +3 \\ \hline \end{array}$$

Name _____

Addition 1-5

Directions: Look at the red numbers and draw that many more flowers in the pot. Count them to get your total.

Example: $3 + 2 = \underline{5}$

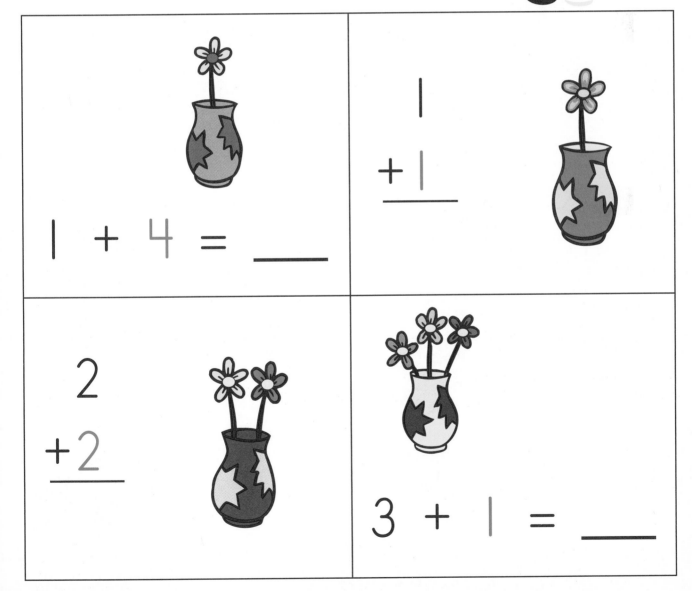

$1 + 4 = \underline{}$

$$\begin{array}{r} 1 \\ +1 \\ \hline \end{array}$$

$$\begin{array}{r} 2 \\ +2 \\ \hline \end{array}$$

$3 + 1 = \underline{}$

Addition 1-5

Directions: Add the numbers. Put your answers in the nests.

Example: 2 + 3 =  5

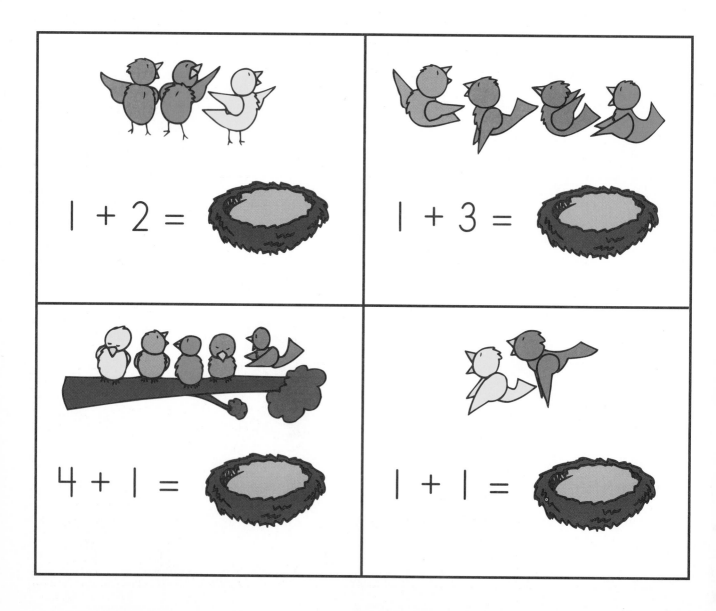

1 + 2 =

1 + 3 =

4 + 1 =

1 + 1 =

Addition 6-10

Directions: Add the numbers. Put your answers in the doghouses.

Example: 4 + 2 = 6

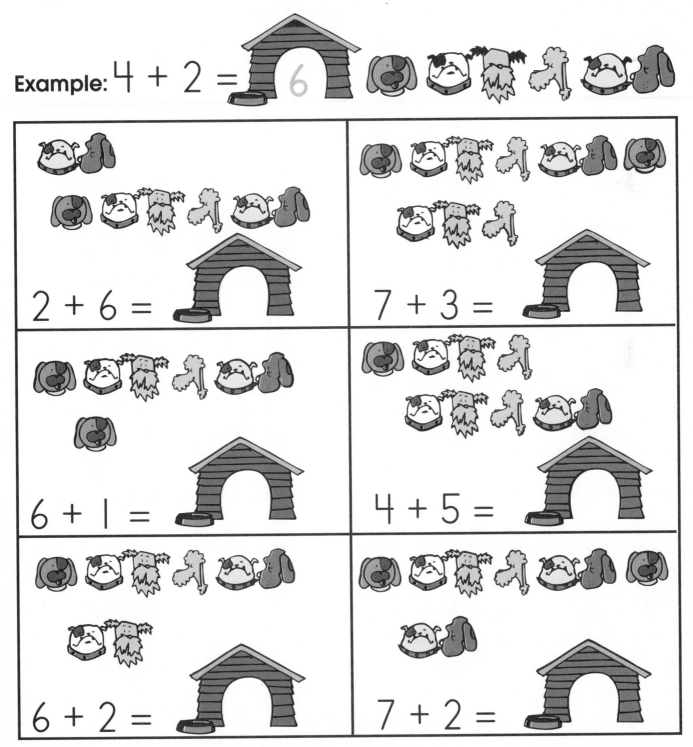

2 + 6 =

7 + 3 =

6 + 1 =

4 + 5 =

6 + 2 =

7 + 2 =

Name _____

Subtraction 1-5

Directions: Subtract the red numbers by crossing out that many flowers in the pot. Count the ones not crossed out to get the total.

Example:

2 – 1 = __1__

5 – 2 = ___

$\begin{array}{r} 4 \\ -2 \\ \hline \end{array}$

$\begin{array}{r} 3 \\ -1 \\ \hline \end{array}$

4 – 3 = ___

Math

Name _____

Subtraction 1-5

Directions: Count the fruit in each bowl. Write your answers on the blanks. Circle the problem that matches your answer.

Name _____

Subtraction 6-10

Directions: Count the flowers. Write your answer on the blank. Circle the problem that matches your answer.

238

Name _____

Addition and Subtraction

Directions: Solve the problems. Remember, addition means "putting together" or adding two or more numbers to find the sum. Subtraction means "taking away" or subtracting one number from another.

1 + 3 = _____   4 – 3 = _____   4 + 5 = _____

6 + 1 = _____   7 – 2 = _____   8 – 4 = _____

9 – 1 = _____   10 – 3 = _____

5 – 2 = _____   6 + 3 = _____

8 + 2 = _____   5 + 5 = _____

Name _____

Addition and Subtraction

Remember, addition means "putting together" or adding two or more numbers to find the sum. Subtraction means "take away" or subtracting one number from another.

Directions: Solve the problems. From your answers, use the code to color the quilt.

Color:
6 = blue
7 = yellow
8 = green
9 = red
10 = orange

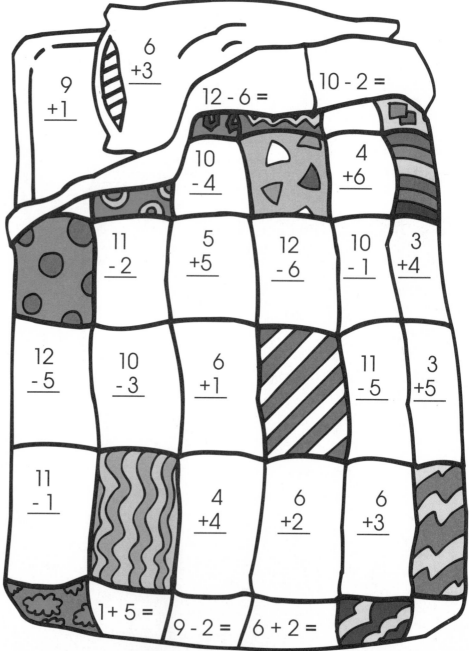

Place Value: Tens and Ones

The place value of a digit, or numeral, is shown by where it is in the number. For example, in the number **23**, **2** has the place value of **tens**, and **3** is ones.

Directions: Count the groups of ten crayons and write the number by the word **tens**. Count the other crayons and write the number by the word **ones**.

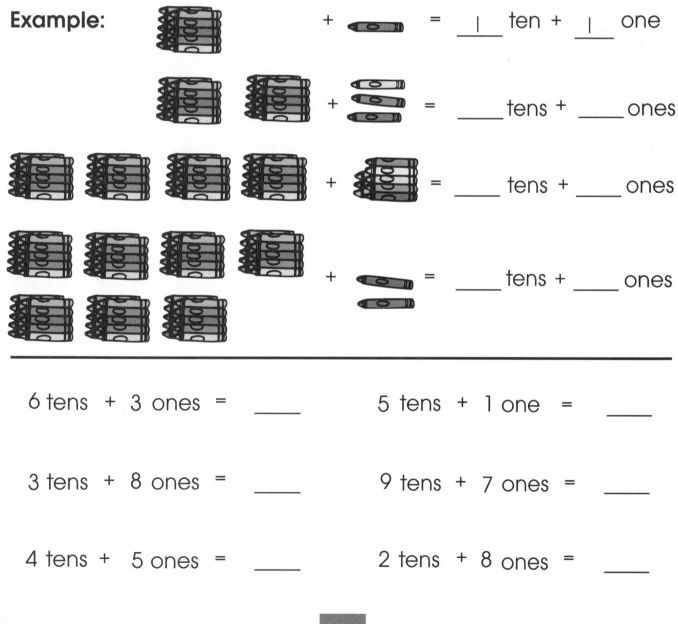

Example: + = _1_ ten + _1_ one

+ = ____ tens + ____ ones

+ = ____ tens + ____ ones

+ = ____ tens + ____ ones

6 tens + 3 ones = ____   5 tens + 1 one = ____

3 tens + 8 ones = ____   9 tens + 7 ones = ____

4 tens + 5 ones = ____   2 tens + 8 ones = ____

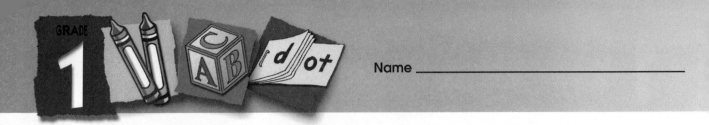

Name _____

Place Value: Tens and Ones

Directions: Count the groups of ten blocks and write the number by the word tens. Count the other blocks and write the number by the word ones.

Example:

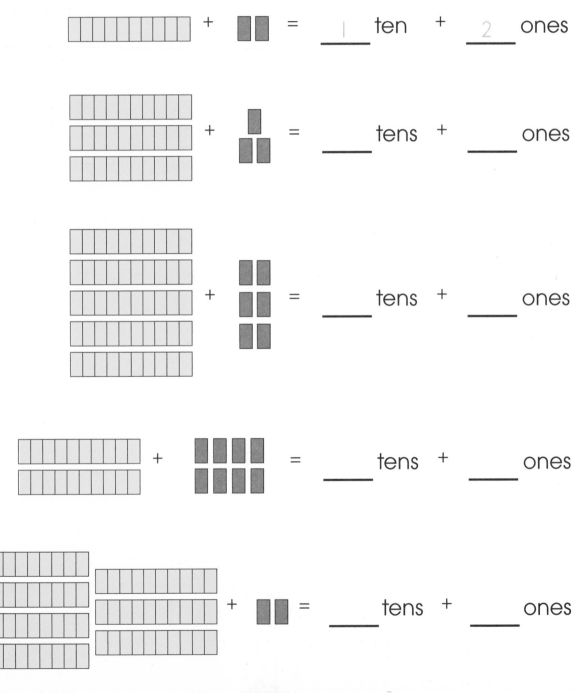

+ = __1__ ten + __2__ ones

+ = _____ tens + _____ ones

+ = _____ tens + _____ ones

+ = _____ tens + _____ ones

+ = _____ tens + _____ ones

Name _____

Place Value: Tens and Ones

Directions: Write the answers in the correct spaces.

		tens	ones		
3 tens, 2 ones		3	2	=	32
3 tens, 7 ones		___	___	=	___
9 tens, 1 one		___	___	=	___
5 tens, 6 ones		___	___	=	___
6 tens, 5 ones		___	___	=	___
6 tens, 8 ones		___	___	=	___
2 tens, 8 ones		___	___	=	___
4 tens, 9 ones		___	___	=	___
1 ten, 4 ones		___	___	=	___
8 tens, 2 ones		___	___	=	___
4 tens, 2 ones		___	___	=	___

28 = ___ tens, ___ ones

64 = ___ tens, ___ ones

56 = ___ tens, ___ ones

72 = ___ tens, ___ ones

38 = ___ tens, ___ ones

17 = ___ ten, ___ ones

63 = ___ tens, ___ ones

12 = ___ ten, ___ ones

Review: Place Value

The place value of each digit, or numeral, is shown by where it is in the number. For example, in the number **123**, **1** has the place value of **hundreds**, **2** is **tens** and **3** is **ones**.

Directions: Count the groups of crayons and add.

Example:

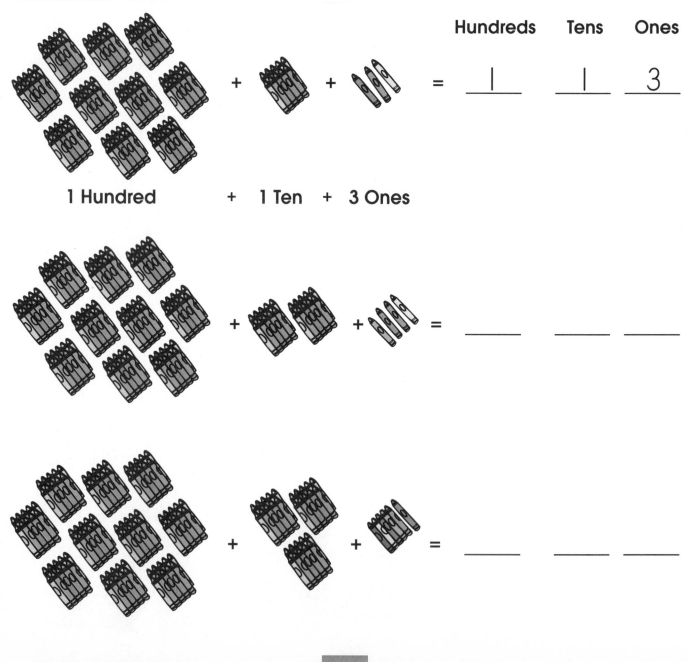

	Hundreds	Tens	Ones
	1	1	3

1 Hundred   +   1 Ten   +   3 Ones

Name _____

Counting by Fives

Directions: Count by fives to draw the path to the playground.

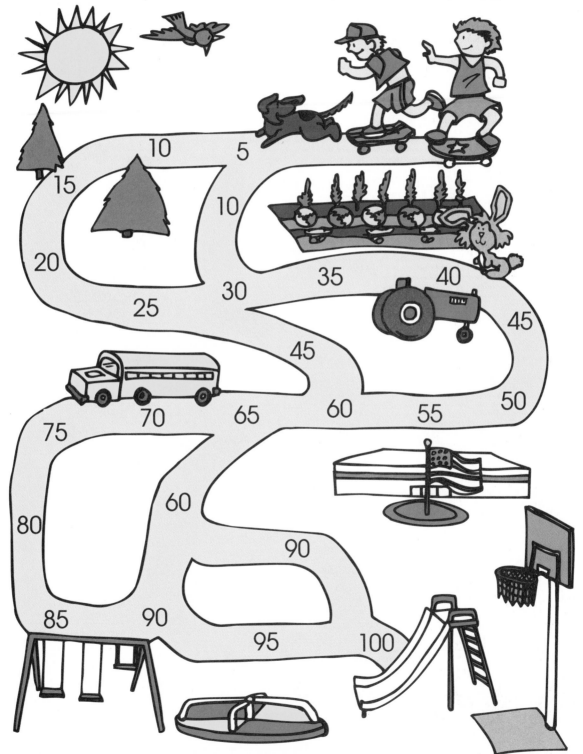

245

Name _____

Counting by Fives

Directions: Use tally marks to count by fives. Write the number next to the tallies.

Example: A tally mark stands for one = I. Five tally marks look like this = ||||

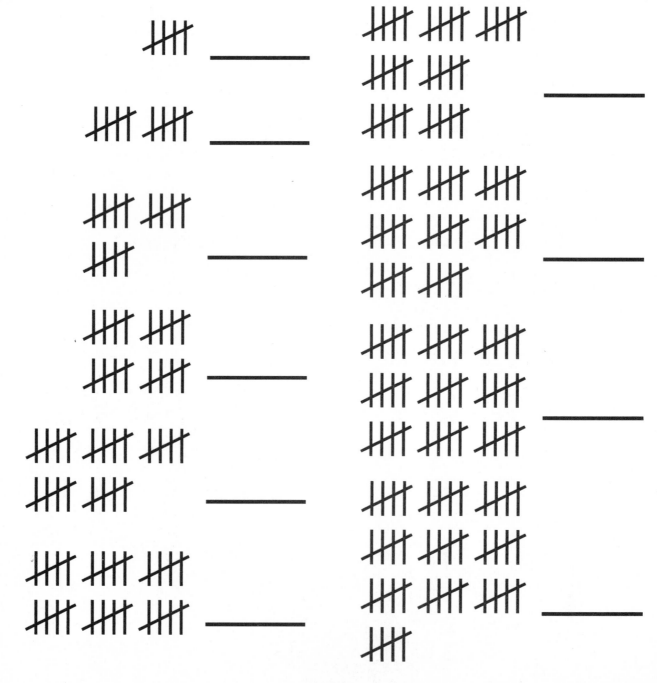

Name _____

Counting by Tens

Directions: Count in order by tens to draw the path the boy takes to the store.

Name _____

Counting by Tens

Directions: Use the groups of 10's to count to 100.

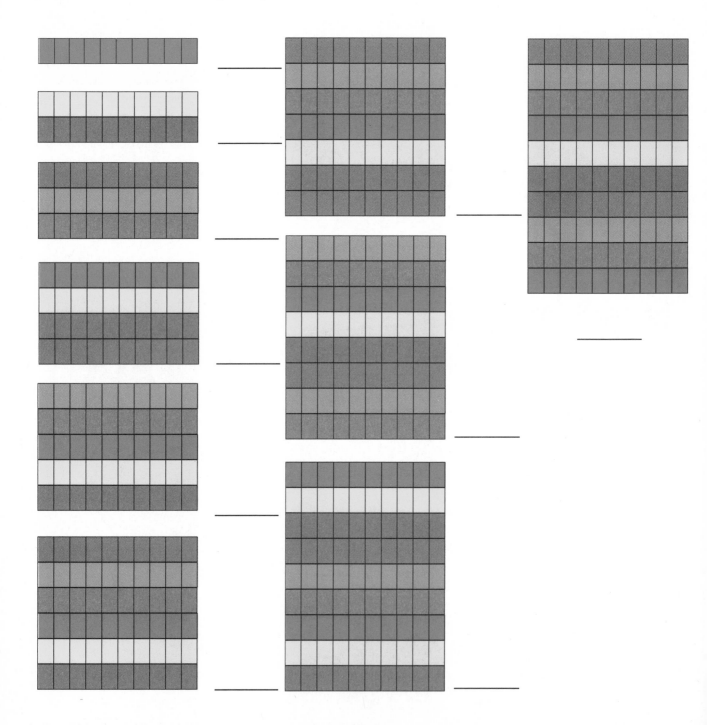

248

Math

Name _____

Addition: 10-15

Directions: Circle groups of ten crayons. Add the remaining ones to make the correct number.

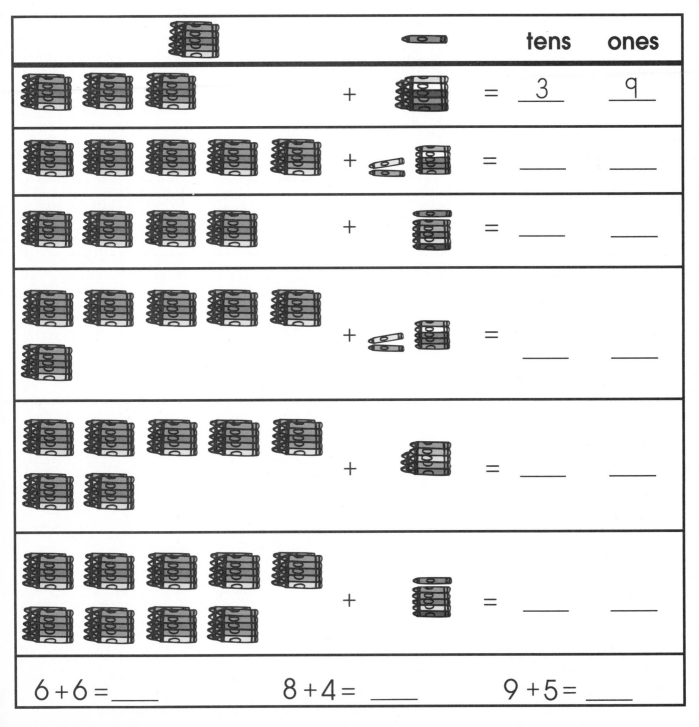

		tens	ones
	+	= 3	9
	+	= ___	___
	+	= ___	___
	+	= ___	___
	+	= ___	___
	+	= ___	___

6 + 6 = ___   8 + 4 = ___   9 + 5 = ___

Subtraction: 10-15

Directions: Count the crayons in each group. Put an **X** through the number of crayons being subtracted. How many are left?

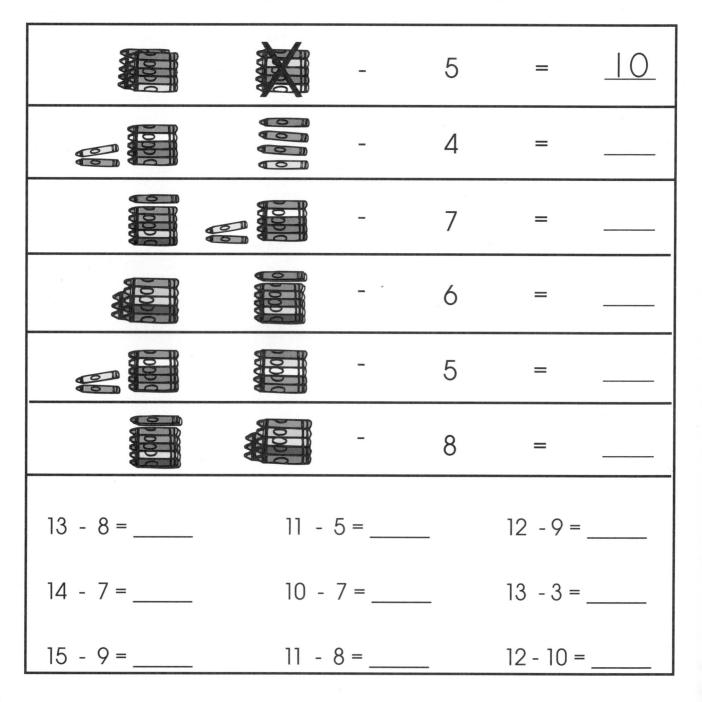

	-	5	=	10
	-	4	=	___
	-	7	=	___
	-	6	=	___
	-	5	=	___
	-	8	=	___

13 - 8 = _____   11 - 5 = _____   12 - 9 = _____

14 - 7 = _____   10 - 7 = _____   13 - 3 = _____

15 - 9 = _____   11 - 8 = _____   12 - 10 = _____

Name _____

Shapes: Square

A square is a figure with four corners and four sides of the same length. This is a square ☐.

Directions: Find the squares and circle them.

Directions: Trace the word. Write the word.

square

Shapes: Circle

A circle is a figure that is round. This is a circle ○.

Directions: Find the circles and put a square around them.

Directions: Trace the word. Write the word.

circle

Name _____

Shapes: Square and Circle

Directions: Practice drawing squares. Trace the samples and make four of your own.

Directions: Practice drawing circles. Trace the samples and make four of your own.

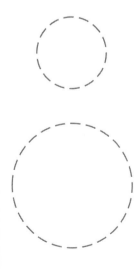

253

Name _____

Shapes: Triangle

A triangle is a figure with three corners and three sides. This is a triangle △.

Directions: Find the triangles and put a circle around them.

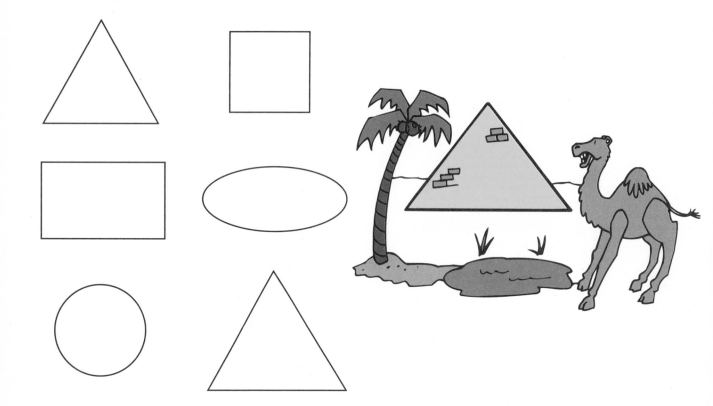

Directions: Trace the word. Write the word.

triangle _____

Shapes: Rectangle

A rectangle is a figure with four corners and four sides. Sides opposite each other are the same length. This is a rectangle ☐.

Directions: Find the rectangles and put a circle around them.

Directions: Trace the word. Write the word.

rectangle

Name _____

Shapes: Triangle and Rectangle

Directions: Practice drawing triangles. Trace the samples and make four of your own.

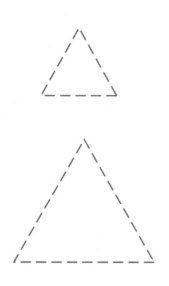

Directions: Practice drawing rectangles. Trace the samples and make four of your own.

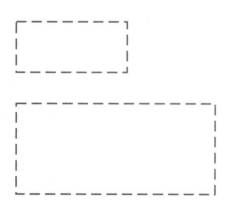

Name _____

Patterns: Rectangles

Directions: In each picture, there is more than one rectangle. Trace each rectangle with a different color crayon. Under each picture, write how many rectangles you found.

_____ rectangles

_____ rectangles

Math

257

Total Basic Skills Grade 1

Patterns: Triangles

Directions: In each picture there is more than one triangle. Trace each triangle with a different color crayon. Under each picture, write how many triangles you found.

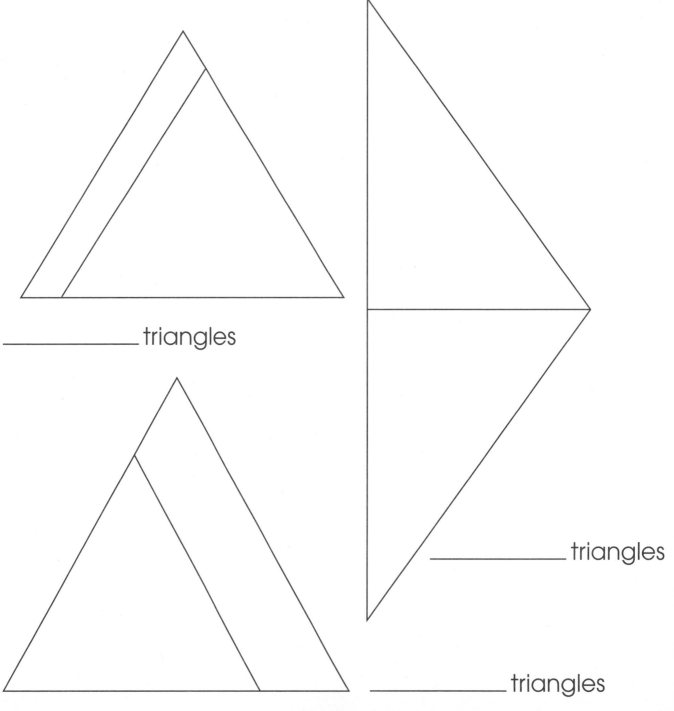

_____ triangles

_____ triangles

_____ triangles

Name _____

Shapes: Oval and Diamond

An oval is an egg-shaped figure. A diamond is a figure with four sides of the same length. Its corners form points at the top, sides and bottom. This is an oval ⬭. This is a diamond ◇.

Directions: Color the ovals red. Color the diamonds blue.

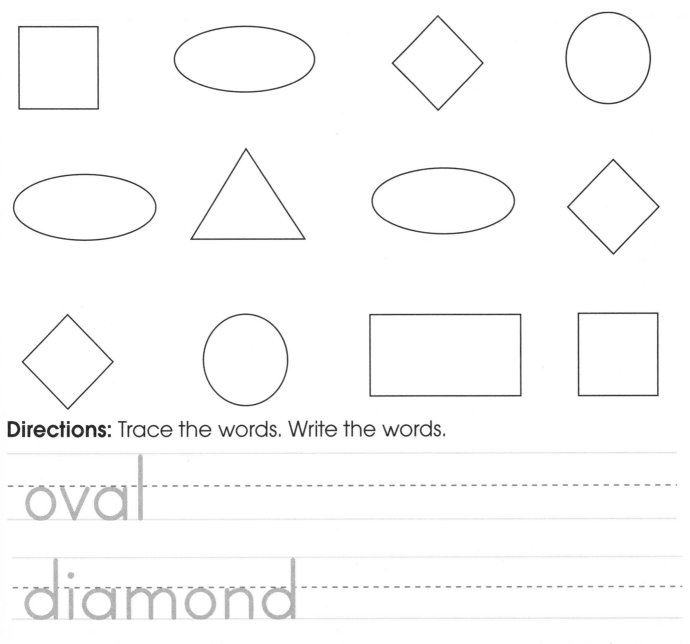

Directions: Trace the words. Write the words.

oval

diamond

Name _____

Shapes: Oval and Diamond

Directions: Practice drawing ovals. Trace the samples and make four of your own.

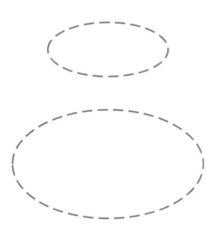

Directions: Practice drawing diamonds. Trace the samples and make four of your own.

Name _____

Following Directions: Shapes and Colors

Directions: Color the squares 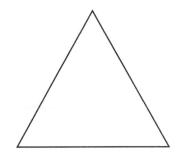 purple.

Directions: Color the heart ♡ blue.

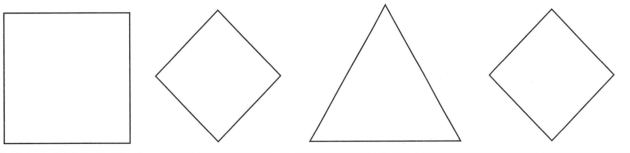

Directions: Color the diamonds ◇ yellow.

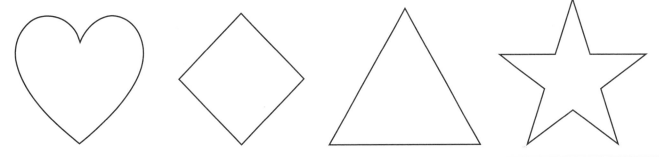

Directions: Color the star ☆ red.

Name _____

Shape Review

Directions: Color the shapes in the picture as shown.

black

red

orange

yellow

blue

green

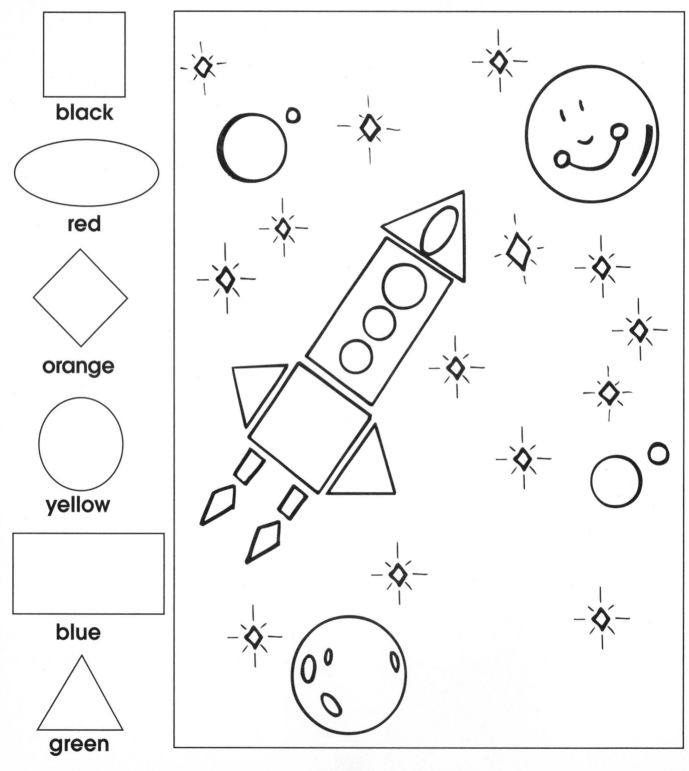

Name _____

Shape Review

Directions: Trace the circles
Trace the squares
Trace the rectangles
Trace the triangles
Trace the ovals
Trace the diamonds

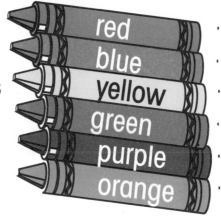

red
blue
yellow
green
purple
orange

Name _____

Classifying: Stars

Help Bob find the stars.

Directions: Color all the stars blue.

How many stars did you and Bob find?_____

264

Classifying: Shapes

Mary and Rudy are taking a trip into space. Help them find the stars, moons, circles and diamonds.

Directions: Color the shapes.

Use yellow for ☆'s.   Use blue for ☾'s.

Use red for ○'s.   Use purple for ◇'s.

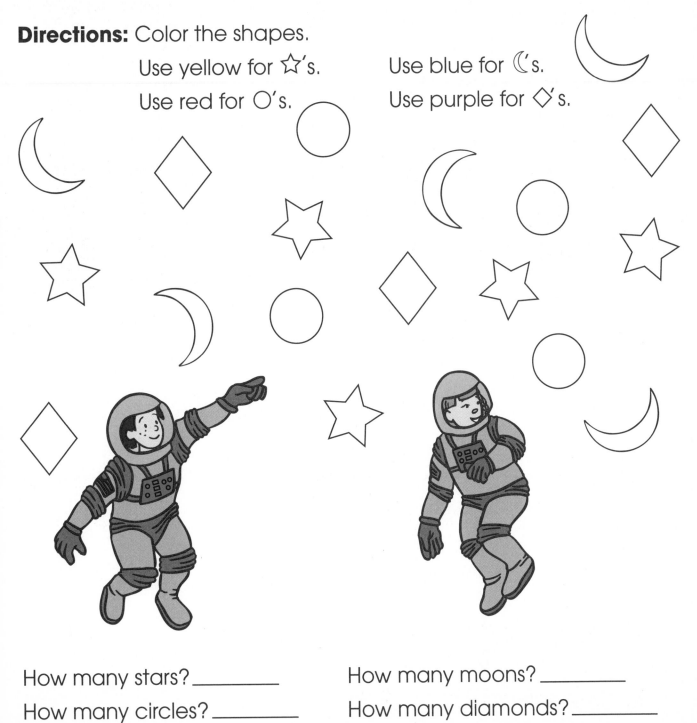

How many stars? _____   How many moons? _____

How many circles? _____   How many diamonds? _____

Name _____

Classifying: Shapes

Directions: Look at the shapes. Answer the questions.

 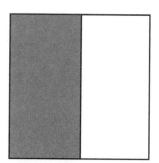  

1. How many all-white shapes? _____

2. How many all-blue shapes? _____

3. How many half-white shapes? _____

4. How many all-blue stars? _____

5. How many all-white circles? _____

6. How many half-blue shapes? _____

GRADE 1

Name _____

Same and Different: Shapes

Directions: Color the shape that looks the same as the first shape in each row.

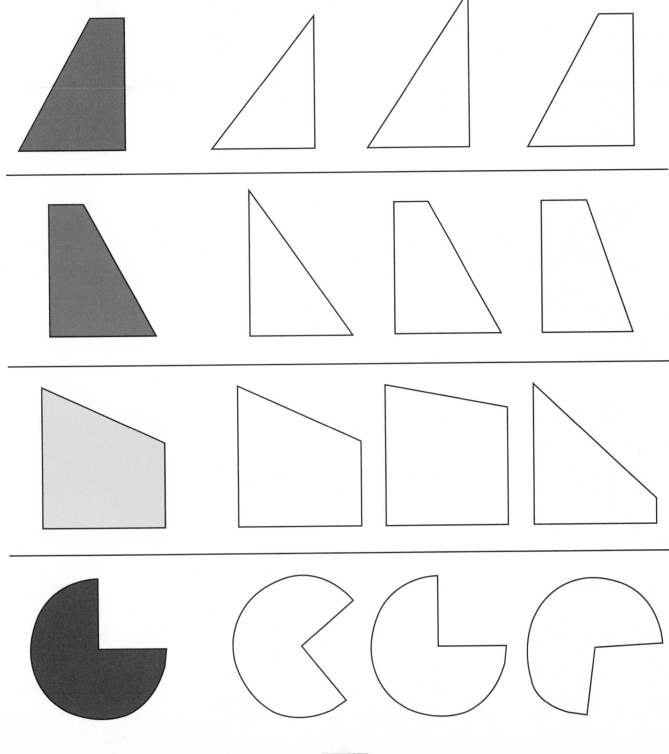

Math

267

Total Basic Skills Grade 1

Same and Different: Shapes

Directions: Draw an **X** on the shapes in each row that do not match the first shape.

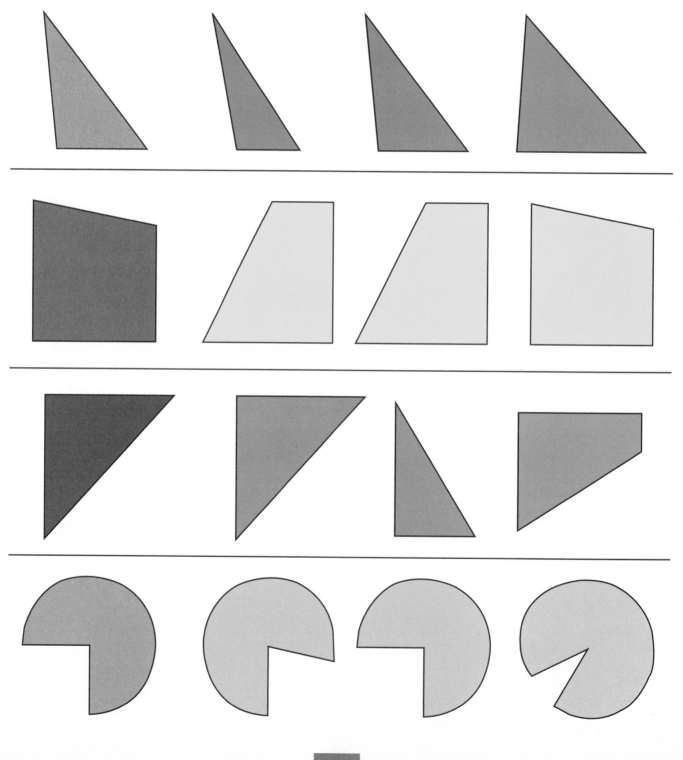

Name _____

Copying: Shapes and Colors

Directions: Color your circle to look the same.

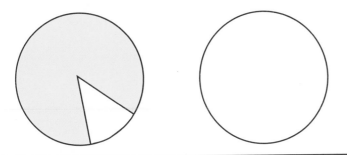

Directions: Color your square to look the same.

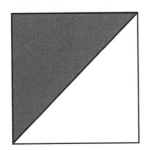

Directions: Trace the triangle. Color it to look the same.

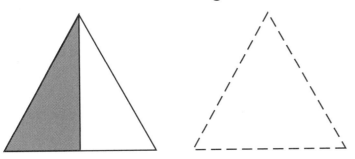

Directions: Trace the star. Color it to look the same.

Name _____

Copying: Shapes and Colors

Directions: Color the second shape the same as the first one. Then draw and color the shape two more times.

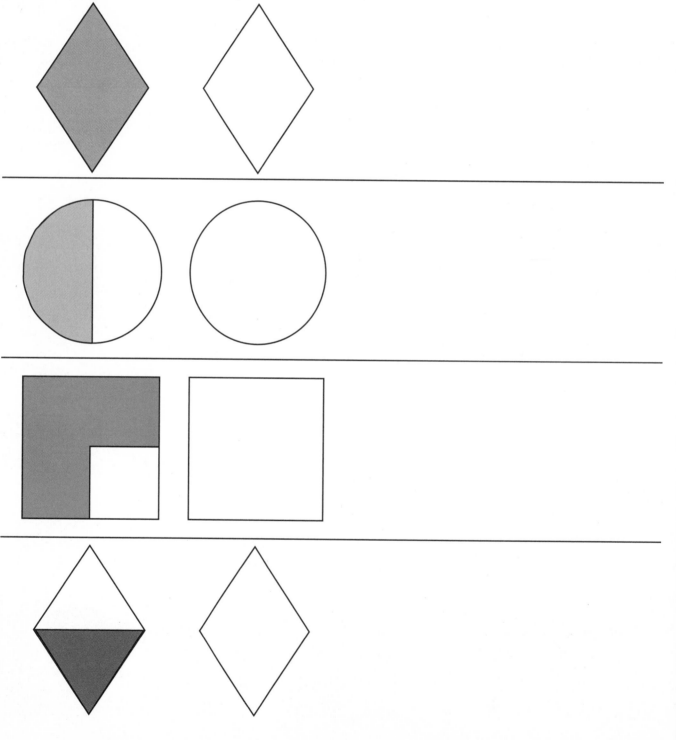

Patterns: Shapes

Directions: Draw a line from the box on the left to the box on the right with the same shape and color pattern.

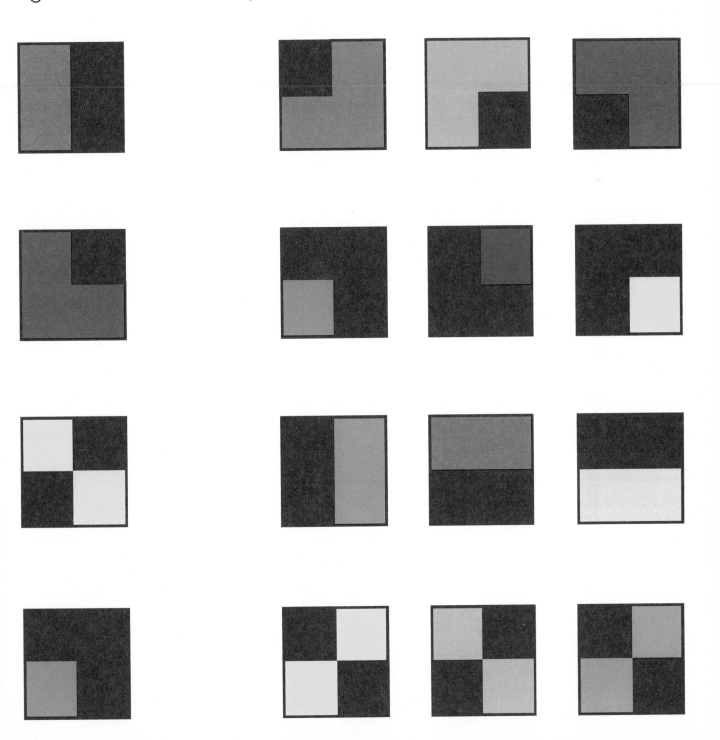

Math

271

Total Basic Skills Grade 1

Name _____

Patterns: Shapes

Directions: Draw a line from the box on the left to the box on the right with the same shape and color pattern.

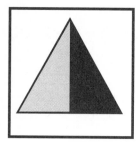

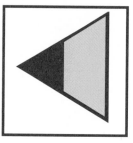

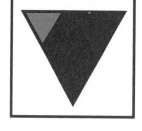

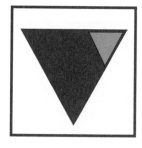

Name _____

Patterns: Find and Copy

Directions: Circle the shape in the middle box that matches the one on the left. Draw another shape with the same pattern in the box on the right.

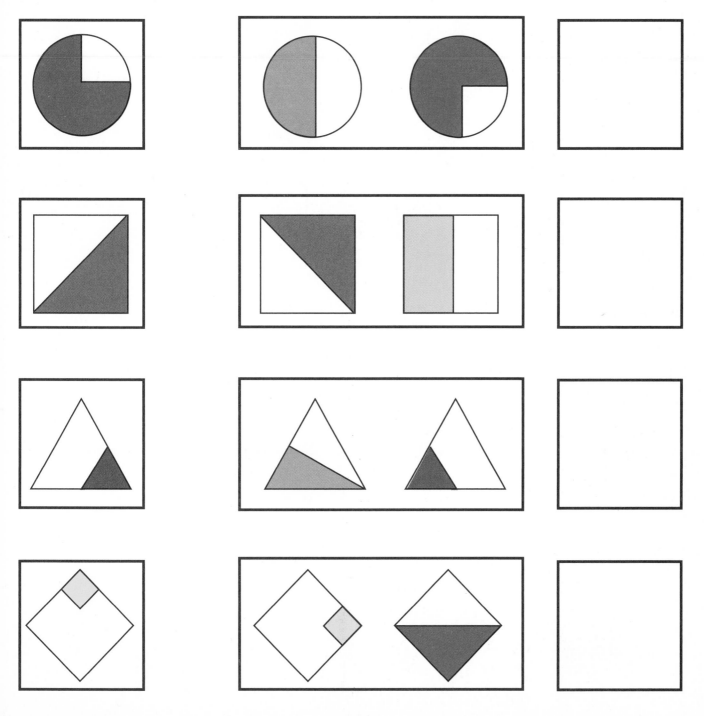

273

Name _____

Patterns

Directions: Draw what comes next in each pattern.

Example:

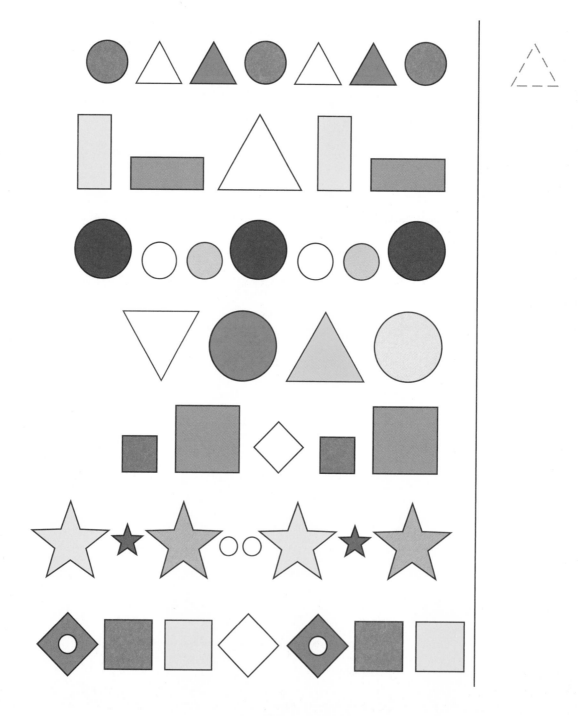

GRADE 1

Name _____

Patterns

Directions: Fill in the missing shape in each row. Then color it.

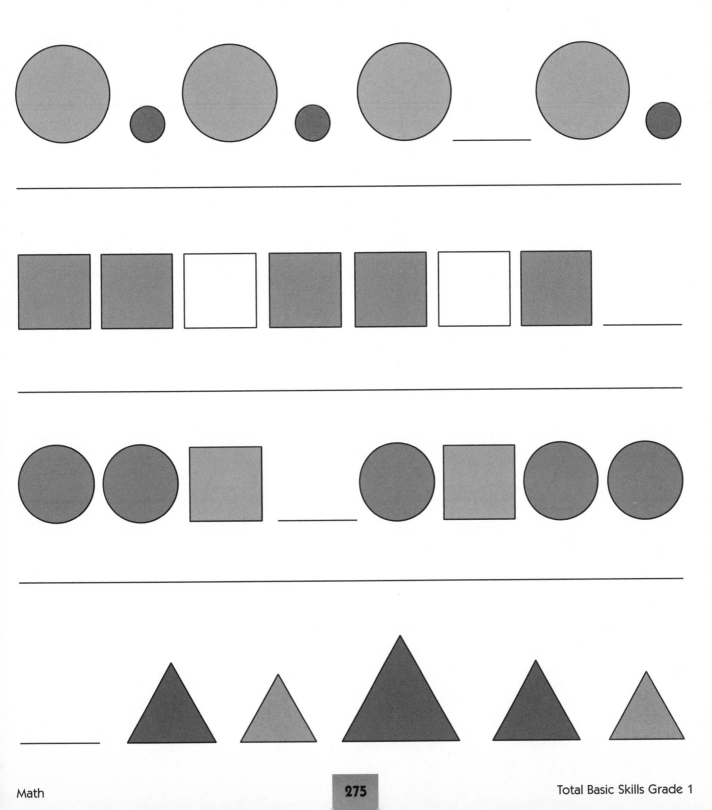

275

Patterns

Directions: Color to complete the patterns.

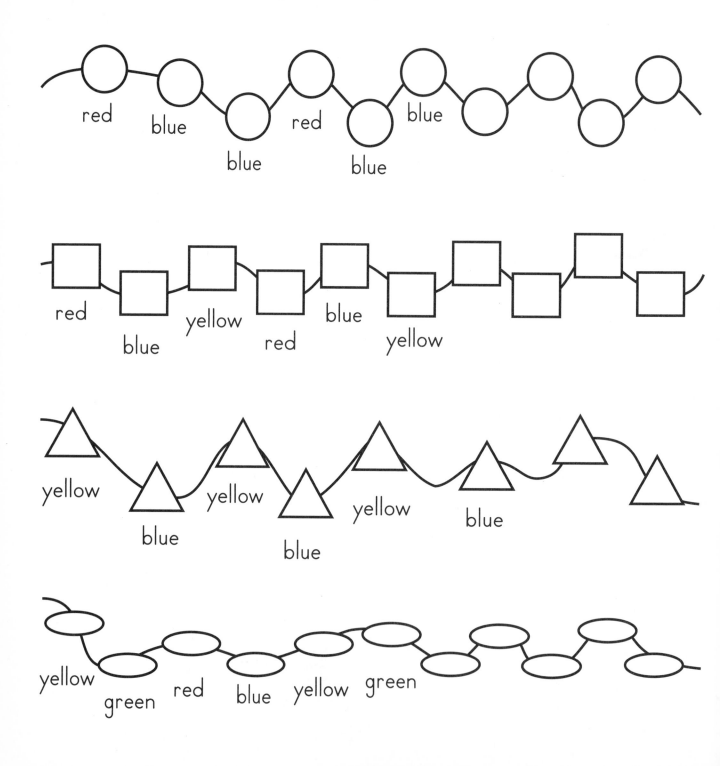

red   blue   blue   red   blue   blue

red   blue   yellow   red   blue   yellow

yellow   blue   yellow   blue   yellow   blue

yellow   green   red   blue   yellow   green

Fractions: Whole and Half

A fraction is a number that names part of a whole, such as $\frac{1}{2}$ or $\frac{3}{4}$.

Directions: Color half of each object.

Example:

Whole apple   Half an apple $\dfrac{1}{2}$

Name _____

Fractions: Halves $\frac{1}{2}$

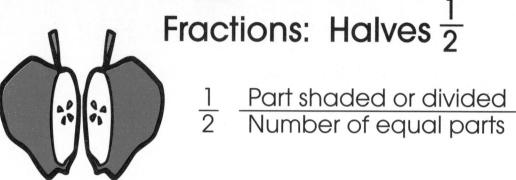

$\frac{1}{2}$ $\dfrac{\text{Part shaded or divided}}{\text{Number of equal parts}}$

Directions: Color only the shapes that show halves.

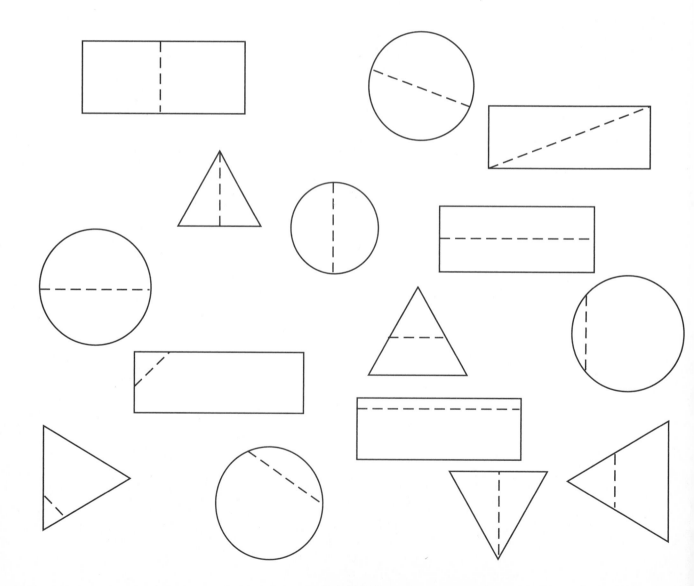

Fractions: Thirds $\frac{1}{3}$

Directions: Circle the objects that have 3 equal parts.

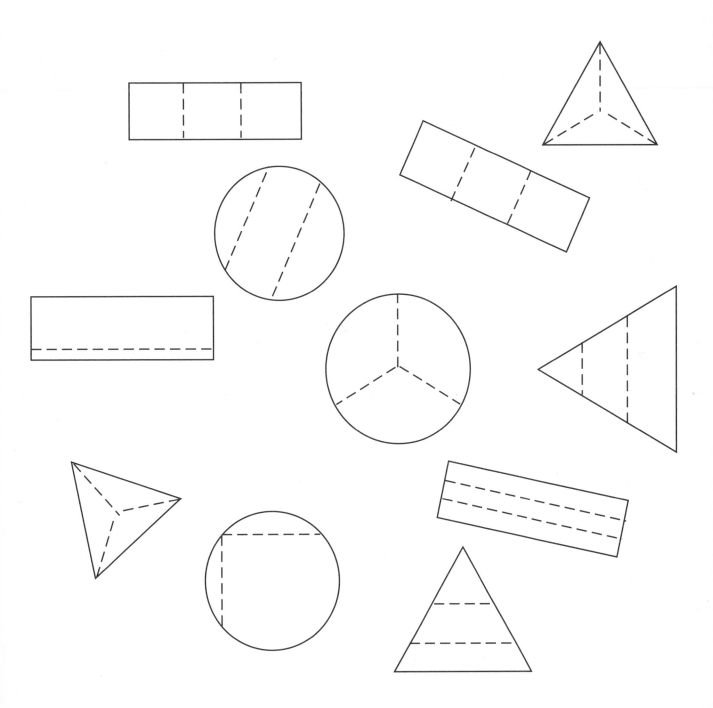

Name _____

Fractions: Fourths $\frac{1}{4}$

Directions: Circle the objects that have four equal parts.

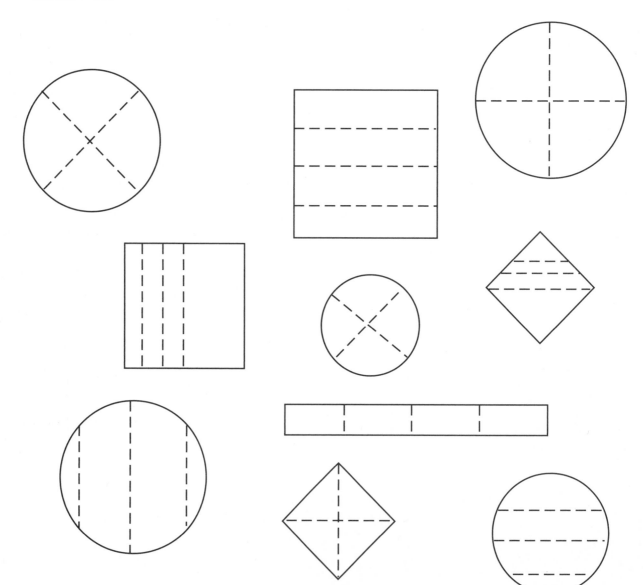

Fractions: Thirds and Fourths

Directions: Each object has 3 equal parts. Color one section.

Directions: Each object has 4 equal parts. Color one section.

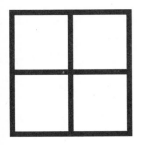

Total Basic Skills Grade 1

Name _____

Review: Fractions

Directions: Count the equal parts, then write the fraction.

Example:

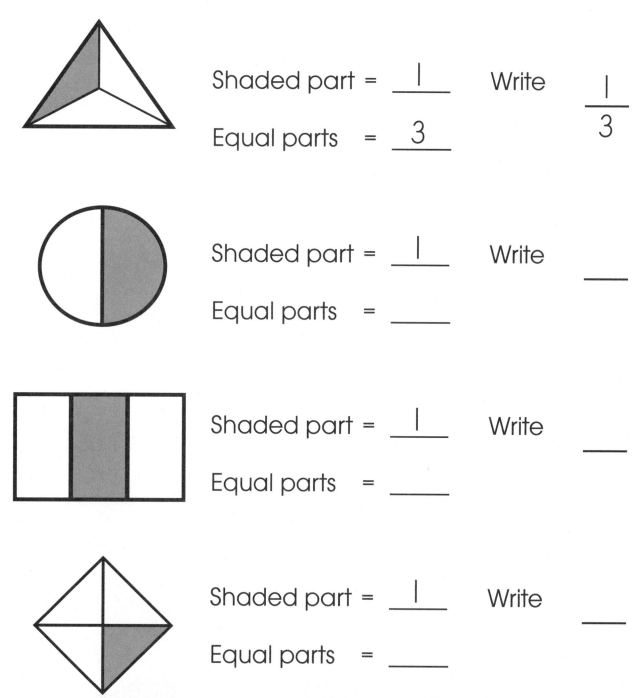

Shaded part = _1_   Write $\frac{1}{3}$

Equal parts = _3_

Shaded part = _1_   Write   ___

Equal parts = ____

Shaded part = _1_   Write   ___

Equal parts = ____

Shaded part = _1_   Write   ___

Equal parts = ____

Name _____

Review

Directions: Write the missing numbers by counting by tens and fives.

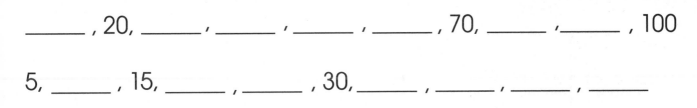

_____ , 20, _____ , _____ , _____ , _____ , 70, _____ , _____ , 100

5, _____ , 15, _____ , _____ , 30, _____ , _____ , _____ , _____

Directions: Color the object with thirds red. Color the object with halves blue. Color the object with fourths green.

Directions: Draw a line to the correct equal part.

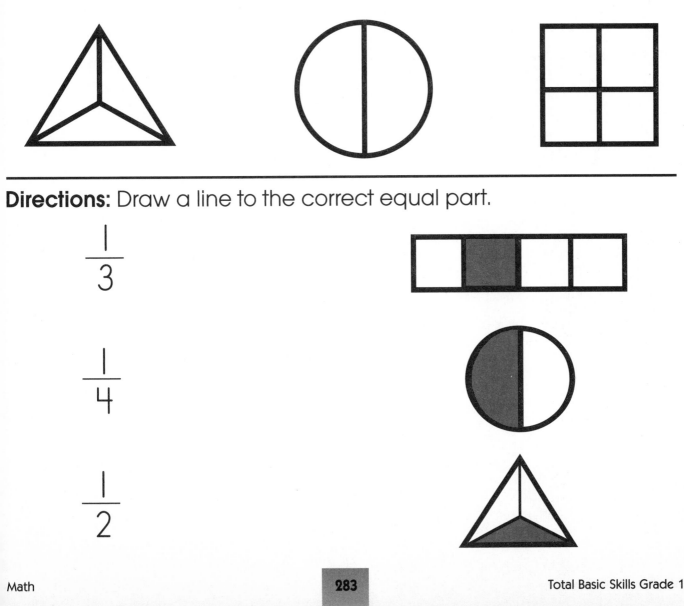

$\frac{1}{3}$

$\frac{1}{4}$

$\frac{1}{2}$

Tracking: Straight Lines

Directions: Draw a straight line from A to B. Use a different color crayon for each line.

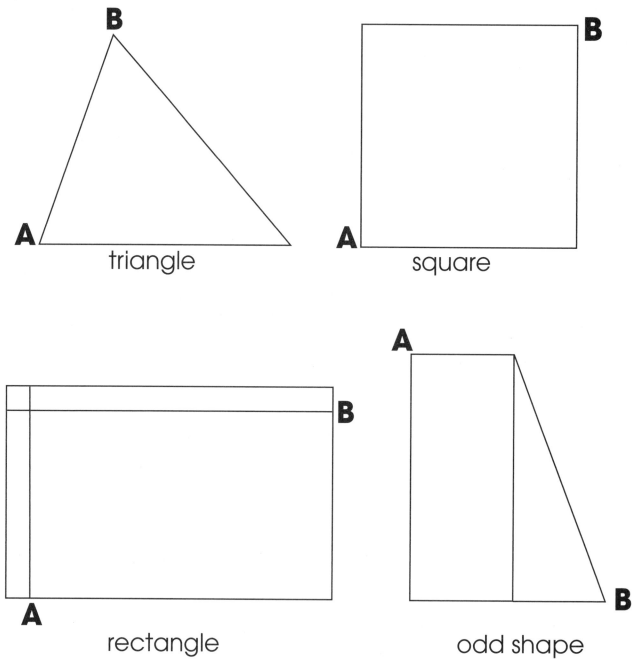

triangle

square

rectangle

odd shape

What shapes do you see hidden in these shapes?

Name _____

Tracking: Different Paths

Directions: Trace three paths from A to B.

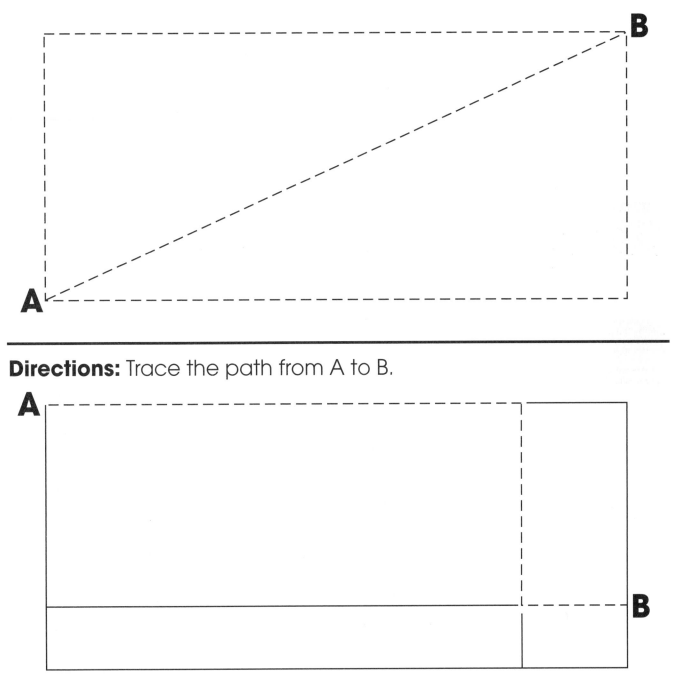

Directions: Trace the path from A to B.

How many corners did you turn? _____

Name _____

Tracking: Different Paths

Help Megan find Mark.

Directions: Trace a path from Megan to Mark.

How many different paths can she follow to reach him? _____

Name _____

Tracking: Different Paths

Directions: Use different colors to trace three paths the bear could take to get the honey.

Name _____

Time: Hour

The short hand of the clock tells the hour. The long hand tells how many minutes after the hour. When the minute hand is on the **12**, it is the beginning of the hour.

Directions: Look at each clock. Write the time.

Example:

__3__ o'clock

____ o'clock  ____ o'clock ____ o'clock ____ o'clock

____ o'clock ____ o'clock ____ o'clock ____ o'clock

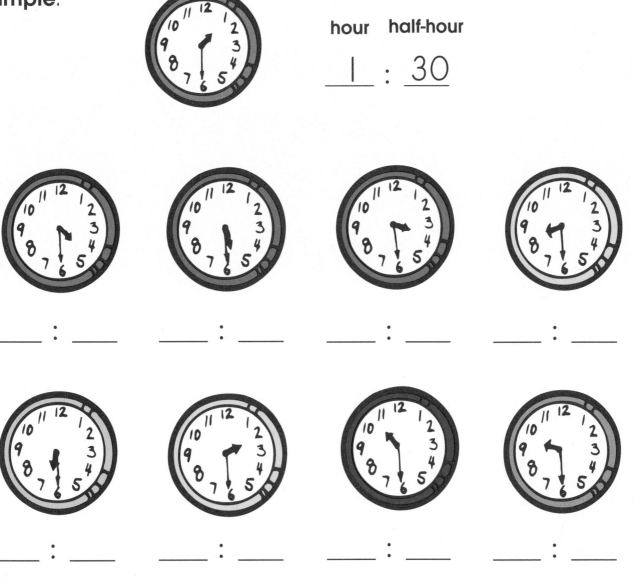

Time: Hour, Half-Hour

The short hand of the clock tells the hour. The long hand tells how many minutes after the hour. When the minute hand is on the **6**, it is on the half-hour. A half-hour is thirty minutes. It is written **:30**, such as **5:30**.

Directions: Look at each clock. Write the time.

Example:

hour   half-hour

<u> 1 </u> : <u>30</u>

___ : ___   ___ : ___   ___ : ___   ___ : ___

___ : ___   ___ : ___   ___ : ___   ___ : ___

Time: Hour, Half-Hour

Directions: Draw the hands on each clock to show the correct time.

   **2:30**      **9:00**

   **7:00**      **4:30**

   **3:00**      **1:30**

Name _____

Time: Counting by Fives

Directions: Fill in the numbers on the clock face. Count by fives around the clock.

There are 60 minutes in one hour.

Name _____

Time: Review

Directions: Look at the time on the digital clocks and draw the hands on the clocks.

Directions: Look at each clock. Write the time.

_____o'clock   _____o'clock

Directions: Look at each clock. Write the time.

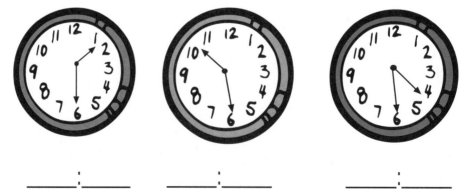

____:____   ____:____   ____:____

Name _____

Review: Time

Directions: Tell what time it is on the clocks.

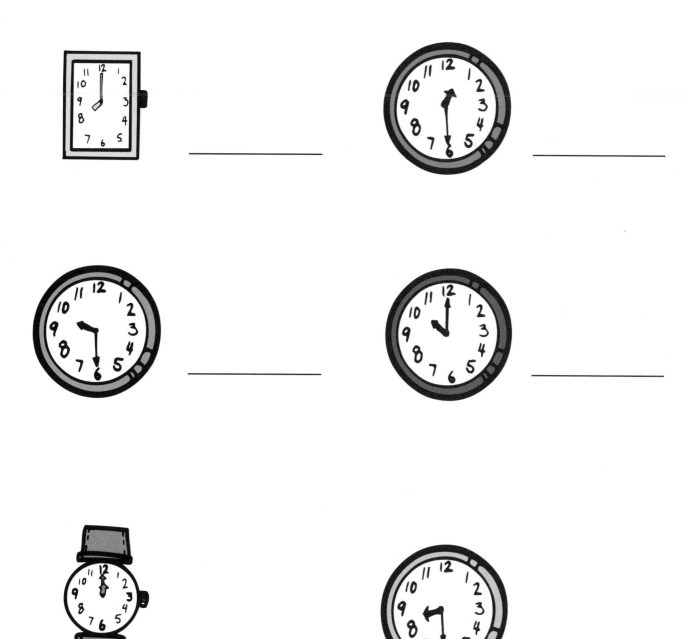

Review: Time

Directions: Match the time on the clock with the digital time.

10:00

5:00

3:00

9:00

2:00

Name _____

Money: Penny and Nickel

A penny is worth one cent. It is written **1¢** or **$.01**. A nickel is worth five cents. It is written **5¢** or **$.05**.

Directions: Count the money and write the answers.

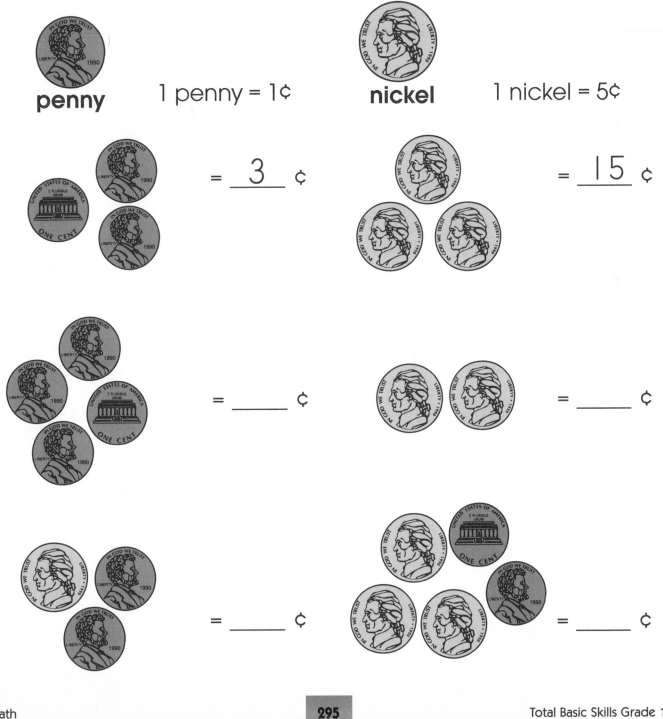

penny   1 penny = 1¢   **nickel**   1 nickel = 5¢

= __3__ ¢   = __15__ ¢

= _____ ¢   = _____ ¢

= _____ ¢   = _____ ¢

Name _____

Money: Penny, Nickel, Dime

A penny is worth one cent. It is written **1¢** or **$.01**. A nickel is worth five cents. It is written **5¢** or **$.05**. A dime is worth ten cents. It is written **10¢** or **$.10**.

Directions: Add the coins pictured and write the total amounts in the blanks.

Example:

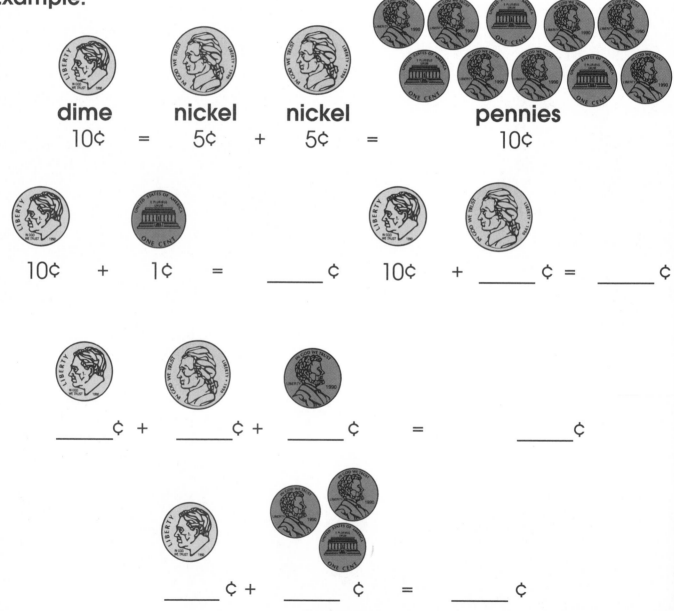

dime   **nickel**   **nickel**   **pennies**

10¢   =   5¢   +   5¢   =   10¢

10¢   +   1¢   =   _____ ¢   10¢   +   _____ ¢   =   _____ ¢

_____ ¢   +   _____ ¢   +   _____ ¢   =   _____ ¢

_____ ¢   +   _____ ¢   =   _____ ¢

Name _____

Money

Directions: Match the amounts in each purse to the price tags.

Name _____

Money: Penny, Nickel, Dime

Directions: Match the correct amount of money with the price of the object.

Name _____

Review

Directions: What time is it?

_____ o'clock

Directions: Draw the hands on each clock.

2:30

7:30

11:00

Directions: How much money?

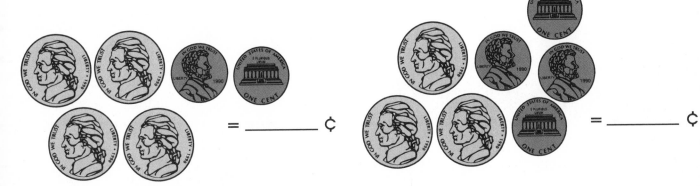

= _____ ¢

= _____ ¢

Directions: Add or subtract.

9 + 3 = _____   6 + 8 = _____   15 - 9 = _____

12 - 8 = _____   12 + 2 = _____   7 + 6 = _____

Name _____

Review

Directions: Follow the instructions.

1. How much money?

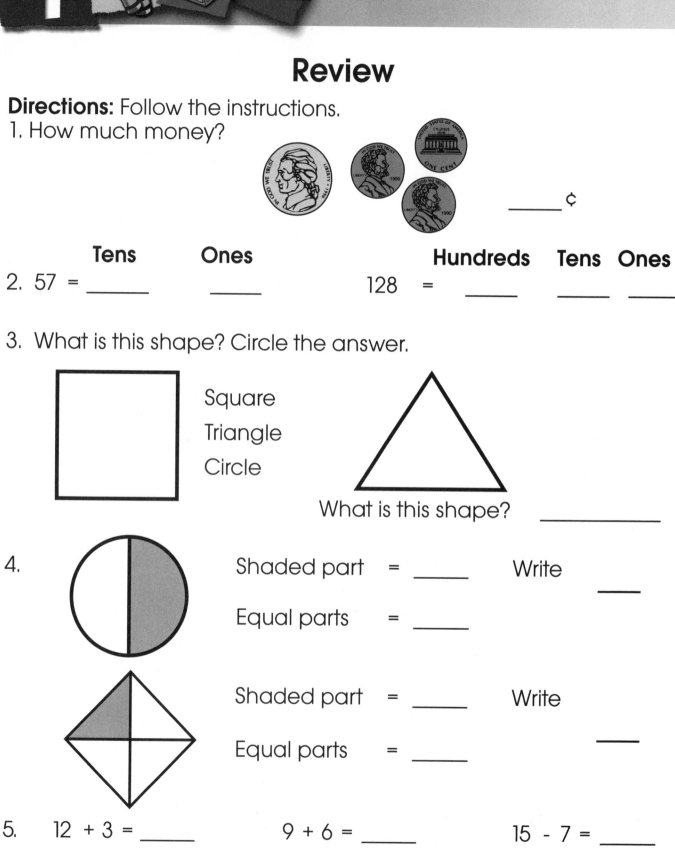

_____ ¢

2.   **Tens   Ones**   **Hundreds   Tens   Ones**

   57 = _____   _____   128 = _____   _____   _____

3. What is this shape? Circle the answer.

Square

Triangle

Circle

What is this shape? _____

4.   Shaded part = _____   Write _____

   Equal parts = _____

   Shaded part = _____   Write _____

   Equal parts = _____

5.   12 + 3 = _____   9 + 6 = _____   15 - 7 = _____

Measurement

A ruler has 12 inches. 12 inches equal 1 foot.

Directions: Cut out the ruler at the bottom of the page. Measure the objects to the nearest inch.

The screwdriver is _____ inches long.

The pencil is _____ inches long.

The pen is _____ inches long.

The fork is _____ inches long.

Cut ✂ _ ✂ _ _

1   2   3   4   5   6   7   8   9   10   11   12

Page is blank for cutting exercise on previous page.

Page 6

Name, Address, Phone

This book belongs to

Answers will vary.

I live at

Answers will vary.

The city I live in is

Answers will vary.

The state I live in is

Answers will vary.

My phone number is

Answers will vary.

Page 7

Review the Alphabet

Directions: Practice writing the letters.

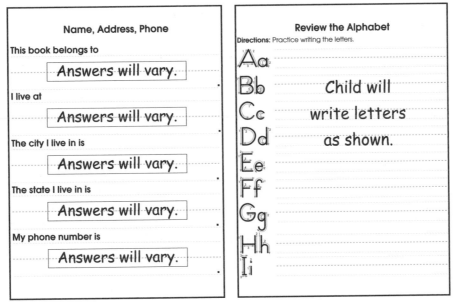

Aa
Bb
Cc
Dd
Ee
Ff
Gg
Hh
Ii

Child will
write letters
as shown.

Page 8

Review the Alphabet

Directions: Practice writing the letters.

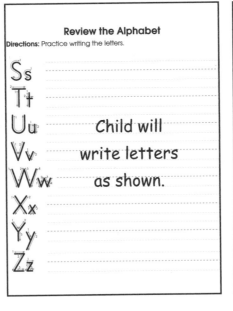

Jj
Kk
Ll
Mm
Nn
Oo
Pp
Qq
Rr

Child will
write letters
as shown.

Page 9

Review the Alphabet

Directions: Practice writing the letters.

Ss
Tt
Uu
Vv
Ww
Xx
Yy
Zz

Child will
write letters
as shown.

Page 10

Letter Recognition

Directions: In each set, match the lower-case letter to the upper-case letter.

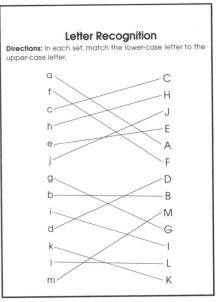

a   C
f   H
c   J
h   E
e   A
j   F

g   D
b   B
i   M
d   G
k   I
l   L
m   K

Page 11

Letter Recognition

Directions: In each set, match the lower-case letter to the upper-case letter.

n   U
s   P
p   R
u   Q
r   N
q   S

t   V
y   O
v   T
o   W
x   Z
w   Y
z   X

Page 12

Beginning Consonants: Bb, Cc, Dd, Ff

Beginning consonants are the sounds that come at the beginning of words. Consonants are the letters b, c, d, f, g, h, j, k, l, m, n, p,q, r, s, t, v, w, x, y and z.

Directions: Say the name of each letter. Say the sound each letter makes. Circle the letters that make the beginning sound for each picture.

Bb   Cc   Dd   Ff

(Bb) Dd   Ff (Cc)   Cc (Dd)   (Ff) Bb

Bb (Dd)   (Ff) Cc   (Cc) Dd   Ff (Bb)

Page 13

Beginning Consonants: Bb, Cc, Dd, Ff

Directions: Say the name of each letter. Say the sound each letter makes. Draw a line from each letter to the picture which begins with that sound.

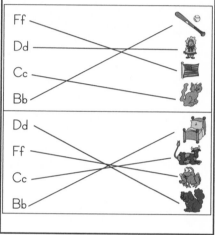

Ff
Dd
Cc
Bb

Dd
Ff
Cc
Bb

Page 14

Beginning Consonants: Gg, Hh, Jj, Kk

Directions: Say the name of each letter. Say the sound each letter makes. Trace the letter pair that makes the beginning sound in each picture.

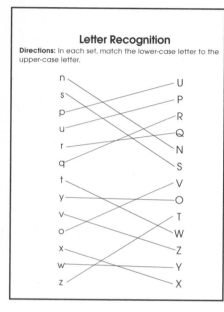

Gg   Hh   Jj   Kk

Kk   **Hh**   Gg   Kk

Gg   Hh   Jj   Gg

Page 15

Beginning Consonants: Gg, Hh, Jj, Kk

Directions: Say the name of each letter. Say the sound each letter makes. Draw a line from each letter pair to the picture which begins with that sound.

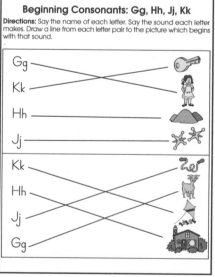

Gg
Kk
Hh
Jj

Kk
Hh
Jj
Gg

Page 16

Beginning Consonants: Ll, Mm, Nn, Pp

Directions: Say the name of each letter. Say the sound each letter makes. Trace the letters. Then draw a line from each letter pair to the picture which begins with that sound.

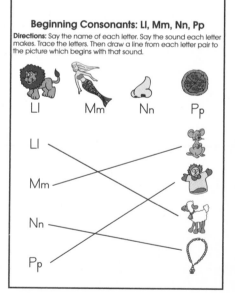

Ll   Mm   Nn   Pp

Ll
Mm
Nn
Pp

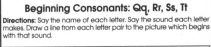

Page 17

Beginning Consonants: Ll, Mm, Nn, Pp

Directions: Say the name of each letter. Say the sound each letter makes. Trace the letter pair that makes the beginning sound in each picture.

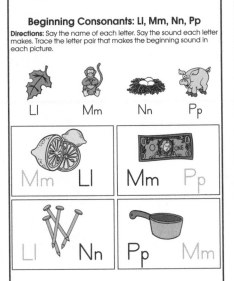

Page 18

Beginning Consonants: Qq, Rr, Ss, Tt

Directions: Say the name of each letter. Say the sound each letter makes. Trace the letter pair in the boxes. Then color the picture which begins with that sound.

Page 19

Beginning Consonants: Qq, Rr, Ss, Tt

Directions: Say the name of each letter. Say the sound each letter makes. Draw a line from each letter pair to the picture which begins with that sound.

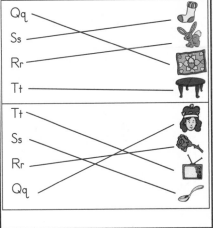

Page 20

Beginning Consonants: Vv, Ww, Xx, Yy, Zz

Directions: Say the name of each letter. Say the sound each letter makes. Trace the letters. Then draw a line from each letter pair to the picture which begins with that sound.

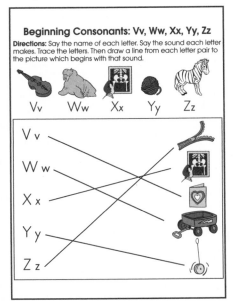

Page 21

Beginning Consonants: Vv, Ww, Xx, Yy, Zz

Directions: Say the name of each letter. Say the sound each letter makes. Then draw a line from each letter pair to the picture which begins with that sound.

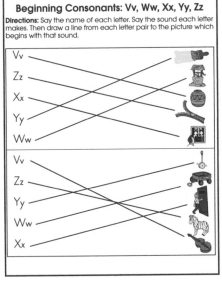

Page 22

Ending Consonants: b, d, f

Ending consonants are the sounds that come at the end of words.
Directions: Say the name of each picture. Then write the letter which makes the **ending** sound for each picture.

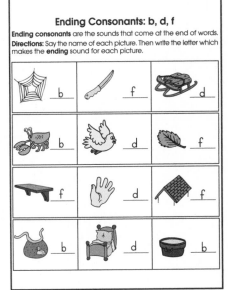

GRADE 1

Page 23

Ending Consonants: g, m, n

Directions: Say the name of each picture. Draw a line from each letter to the pictures which end with that sound.

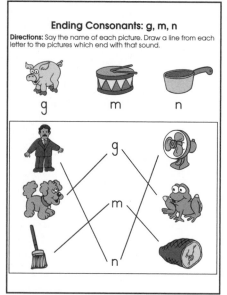

g   m   n

Page 24

Ending Consonants: k, l, p

Directions: Trace the letters in each row. Say the name of each picture. Then color the pictures in each row which end with that sound.

k

l

p

Page 25

Ending Consonants: r, s, t, x

Directions: Say the name of each picture. Then circle the ending sound for each picture.

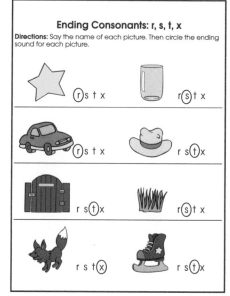

(r) s t x   r (s) t x

(r) s t x   r s (t) x

r s (t) x   r (s) t x

r s t (x)   r s (t) x

Page 26

Short Vowels

Vowels are the letters **a, e, i, o** and **u**. Short **a** is the sound you hear in **ant**. Short **e** is the sound you hear in **elephant**. Short **i** is the sound you hear in **igloo**. Short **o** is the sound you hear in **octopus**. Short **u** is the sound you hear in **umbrella**.

Directions: Say the short vowel sound at the beginning of each row. Say the name of each picture. Then color the pictures which have the same short vowel sounds as that letter.

ă
ĕ
ĭ
ŏ
ŭ

Page 27

Short Vowel Sounds

Directions: In each box are three pictures. The words that name the pictures have missing letters. Write **a, e, i, o** or **u** to finish the words.

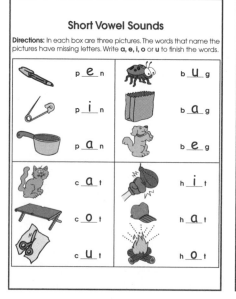

p e n   b u g
p i n   b a g
p a n   b e g

c a t   h i t
c o t   h a t
c u t   h o t

Page 28

Long Vowels

Vowels are the letters **a, e, i, o** and **u**. Long vowel sounds say their own names. Long **a** is the sound you hear in **hay**. Long **e** is the sound you hear in **me**. Long **i** is the sound you hear in **pie**. Long **o** is the sound you hear in **no**. Long **u** is the sound you hear in **cute**.

Directions: Say the long vowel sound at the beginning of each row. Say the name of each picture. Color the pictures in each row that have the same long vowel sound as that letter.

ā
ē
ī
ō
ū

Total Basic Skills Grade 1   306   Answer Key

Page 29

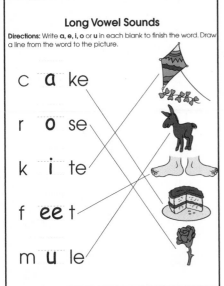

Long Vowel Sounds

Directions: Write **a, e, i, o** or **u** in each blank to finish the word. Draw a line from the word to the picture.

c **a** ke

r **o** se

k **i** te

f **ee** t

m **u** le

Page 30

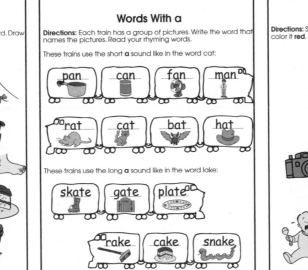

Words With a

Directions: Each train has a group of pictures. Write the word that names the pictures. Read your rhyming words.

These trains use the short **a** sound like in the word cat:

pan   can   fan   man

rat   cat   bat   hat

These trains use the long **a** sound like in the word lake:

skate   gate   plate

rake   cake   snake

Page 31

Short and Long Aa

Directions: Say the name of each picture. If it has the short **a** sound, color it **red**. If it has the long **a** sound, color it **yellow**.

ă   ā

Page 32

Words with e

Directions: Short **e** sounds like the **e** in hen. Long **e** sounds like the **e** in bee. Look at the pictures. If the word has a short **e** sound, draw a line to the **hen** with your **red** crayon. If the word has a long **e** sound, draw a line to the **bee** with your **green** crayon.

hen   bee

Page 33

Short and Long Ee

Directions: Say the name of each picture. Circle the pictures which have the short **e** sound. Draw a triangle around the pictures which have the long **e** sound.

ĕ   ē

Page 34

Words with i

Directions: Short **i** sounds like the **i** in pig. Long **i** sounds like the **i** in kite. Draw a circle around the words with the short **i** sound. Draw an **X** on the words with the long **i** sound.

pin   five   pig

slide   kite   lid

tie   bib   pie

Page 35

Short and Long Ii

Directions: Say the name of each picture. If it has the short **i** sound, color it **yellow**. If it has the long **i** sound, color it **red**.

Page 36

Words With o

Directions: The short **o** sounds like the **o** in dog. Long **o** sounds like the **o** in rope. Draw a line from the picture to the word that names it. Draw a circle around the word if it has a short **o** sound.

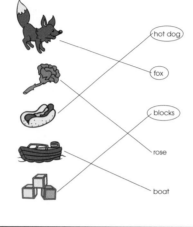

hot dog
fox
blocks
rose
boat

Page 37

Short and Long Oo

Directions: Say the name of each picture. If the picture has the long **o** sound, write a **green L** on the blank. If the picture has the short **o** sound, write a **red S** on the blank.

L   S
S   S   L
L   S   L

Page 38

Words With u

Directions: The short **u** sounds like the **u** in bug. The long **u** sounds like the **u** in blue. Draw a circle around the words with short **u**. Draw an **X** on the words with long **u**.

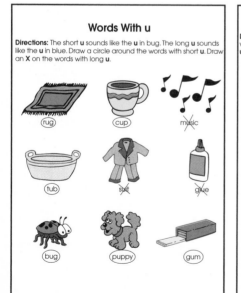

rug   cup   music
tub   suit   glue
bug   puppy   gum

Page 39

Short and Long Uu

Directions: Say the name of each picture. If it has the long **u** sound, write a **u** in the **unicorn** column. If it has the short **u** sound, write a **u** in the **umbrella** column.

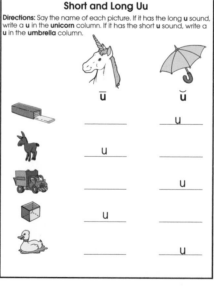

ū   ŭ

_____   u
u   _____
_____   u
u   _____
_____   u

Page 40

Super Silent E

When you add an **e** to the end of some words, the vowel changes from a short vowel sound to a long vowel sound. The **e** is silent.
Example: rip + e = ripe.

Directions: Say the word under the first picture in each pair. Then add an **e** to the word under the next picture. Say the new word.

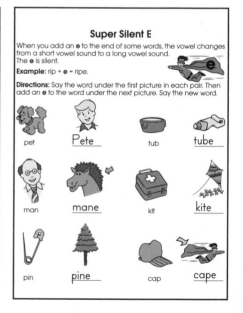

pet   Pete   tub   tube
man   mane   kit   kite
pin   pine   cap   cape

Page 41

Consonant Blends

Consonant blends are two or more consonant sounds together in a word. The blend is made by combining the consonant sounds.

Example: <u>fl</u>oor

Directions: The name of each picture begins with a **blend**. Circle the beginning blend for each picture.

Page 42

Consonant Blends

Directions: The beginning blend for each word is missing. Fill in the correct blend to finish the word. Draw a line from the word to the picture.

tr
fr
cr
dr
br
pr

ain
og
ab
um
ush
esent

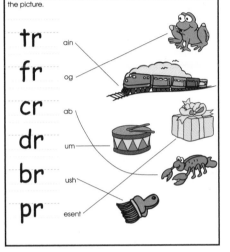

Page 43

Consonant Blends

Directions: Draw a line from the picture to the blend that begins its word.

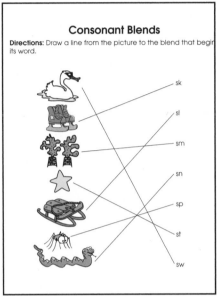

sk
sl
sm
sn
sp
st
sw

Page 44

Consonant Blends

Directions: Look at the first picture in each row. Circle the pictures in the row that begin with the same sound.

chair
shell
thumb
wheel

Page 45

Beginning Blends

Directions: Say the blend for each word as you search for it.

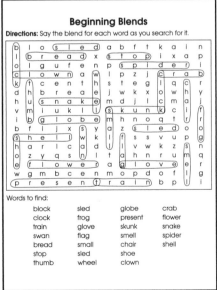

Words to find:

block	sled	globe	crab
clock	frog	present	flower
train	glove	skunk	snake
swan	flag	smell	spider
bread	small	chair	shell
stop	sled	shoe	
thumb	wheel	clown	

Page 46

Ending Consonant Blends

Directions: Write **lt** or **ft** to complete the words.

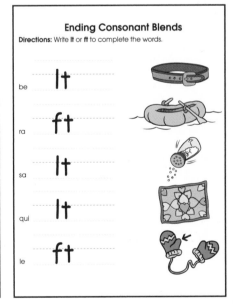

be   lt
ra   ft
sa   lt
qui   lt
le   ft

Page 47

Ending Consonant Blends

Directions: Draw a line from the picture to the blend that end the word.

lf

lk

sk

st

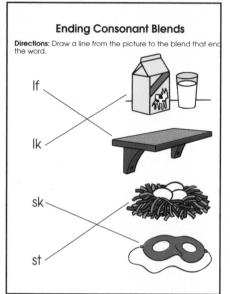

Page 48

Ending Consonant Blends

Directions: Every juke box has a word ending and a list of letters. Add each of the letters to the word ending to make rhyming words.

___and
b **and**
h **and**
l **and**
s **and**

___ent
b **ent**
d **ent**
t **ent**
w **ent**

___ump
b **ump**
d **ump**
j **ump**
p **ump**

___ink
p **ink**
s **ink**
l **ink**
th **ink**

___ing
r **ing**
s **ing**
st **ing**
k **ing**

___ank
b **ank**
r **ank**
s **ank**
t **ank**

Page 49

Ending Consonant Blends

Directions: Say the blend for each word as you search for it.

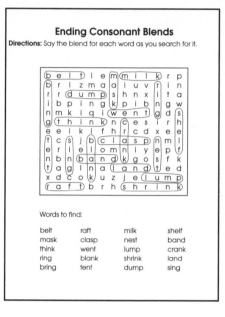

Words to find:

belt	raft	milk	shelf
mask	clasp	nest	band
think	went	lump	crank
ring	blank	shrink	land
bring	tent	dump	sing

Page 50

Rhyming Words

Rhyming words are words that sound alike at the end of the word. **Cat** and **hat** rhyme.

Directions: Draw a circle around each word pair that rhymes. Draw an **X** on each pair that does not rhyme.

Example:

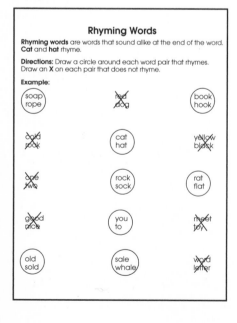

Page 51

Rhyming Words

Rhyming words are words that sound alike at the end of the word.

Directions: Draw a line to match the pictures that rhyme. Write two of your own rhyming word pairs below.

Answers

will vary.

Page 52

ABC Order

Directions: **Abc** order is the order in which letters come in the alphabet. Draw a line to connect the dots. Follow the letters in **abc** order. Then color the picture.

Page 53

ABC Order

Directions: Draw a line to connect the dots. Follow the letters in abc order. Then color the picture.

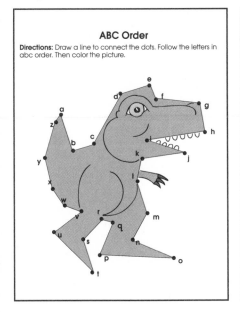

Page 54

ABC Order

Directions: Circle the first letter of each word. Then put each pair of the words in abc order.

bird
car

moon
two

fan
nest

card
dog

bike
pig

pie
sun

Page 55

ABC Order

Directions: Look at the words in each box. Circle the word that comes first in abc order.

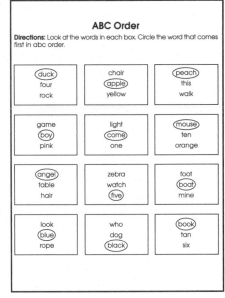

(duck) four rock	chair (apple) yellow	(peach) this walk
game (boy) pink	light (come) one	(mouse) ten orange
(angel) table hair	zebra watch (five)	foot (boat) mine
look (blue) rope	who dog (black)	(book) tan six

Page 56

Compound Words

Compound words are two words that are put together to make one new word.

Directions: Look at the pictures and the two words that are next to each other. Put the words together to make a new word. Write the new word.

Example:

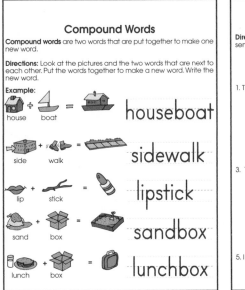

🏠 + ⛵ = 🚤 **houseboat**
house boat

 + = **sidewalk**
side walk

 + = **lipstick**
lip stick

 + = **sandbox**
sand box

 + = **lunchbox**
lunch box

Page 57

Compound Words

Directions: Circle the compound word which completes each sentence. Write each word on the lines.

1. The **mailman** brings us letters.
   (mailman) snowman

2. A **sunflower** grows tall.
   sunlight (sunflower)

3. The snow falls **outside**
   (outside) inside

4. A **raindrop** fell on my head.
   (raindrop) rainbow

5. I put the letter in a **mailbox**
   (mailbox) shoebox

Page 58

Names

You are a special person. Your name begins with a capital letter. We put a capital letter at the beginning of people's names because they are special.

Directions: Write your name. Did you remember to use a capital letter?

Answers will vary.

Directions: Write each person's name. Use a capital letter at the beginning.

Ted — Ted

Katie — Katie

Mike — Mike

Tim — Tim

Write a friend's name. Use a capital letter at the beginning.

Answers will vary.

Page 59

Names: Days of the Week

The days of the week begin with capital letters.

Directions: Write the days of the week in the spaces below. Put them in order. Be sure to start with capital letters.

Tuesday
Saturday
Monday
Friday
Thursday
Sunday
Wednesday

	Sunday
	Monday
	Tuesday
	Wednesday
	Thursday
	Friday
	Saturday

Page 60

Names: Months of the Year

The months of the year begin with capital letters.

Directions: Write the months of the year in order on the calendar below. Be sure to use capital letters.

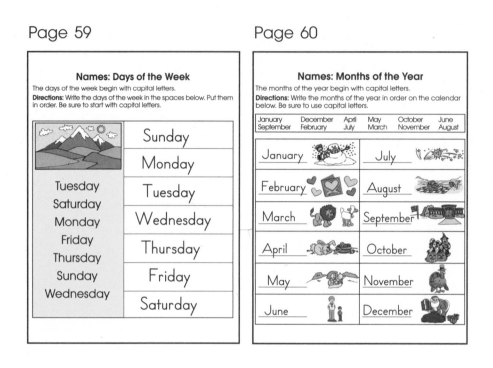

January September	December February	April July	May March	October November	June August

January		July	
February		August	
March		September	
April		October	
May		November	
June		December	

Page 61

More Than One

Directions: An **s** at the end of a word often means there is more than one. Look at each picture. Circle the correct word. Write the word on the line.

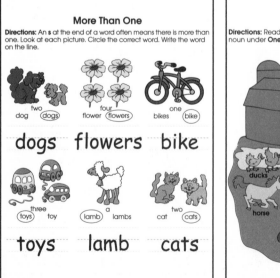

two dog (dogs)
four flower (flowers)
one bikes (bike)

dogs **flowers** **bike**

three (toys) toy
a (lamb) lambs
two cat (cats)

toys **lamb** **cats**

Page 62

More Than One

Directions: Read the nouns under the pictures. Then write each noun under **One** or **More Than One**.

One

barn

wagon

horse

More Than One

cows

pigs

ducks

Page 64

More Than One

Directions: Choose the word which completes each sentence. Write each word on the line.

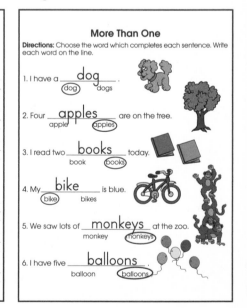

1. I have a ___dog___ . (dog) dogs

2. Four ___apples___ are on the tree. apple (apples)

3. I read two ___books___ today. book (books)

4. My ___bike___ is blue. (bike) bikes

5. We saw lots of ___monkeys___ at the zoo. monkey (monkeys)

6. I have five ___balloons___ . balloon (balloons)

Page 65

Riddles

Directions: Read the word. Trace and write it on the line. Then draw a line from the riddle to the animal it tells about.

long **long long**

I am very big.
I lived a long, long time ago.
What am I?

My neck is very long.
I eat leaves from trees.
What am I?

I have long ears.
I hop very fast.
What am I?

giraffe

rabbit

dinosaur

Page 66

Riddles

Directions: Read the word and write it on the line. Then read each riddle and draw a line to the picture and word that tells about it.

house
house

kitten
kitten

flower
flower

pony
pony

I like to play.
I am little. I am soft.
What am I?
house

I am big.
You live in me.
What am I?
kitten

I am pretty.
I am green and yellow.
What am I?
flower

I can jump. I can run.
I am brown.
What am I?
pony

Page 67

Riddles

Directions: Write a word from the box to answer each riddle.

| ice cream | book | chair | sun |

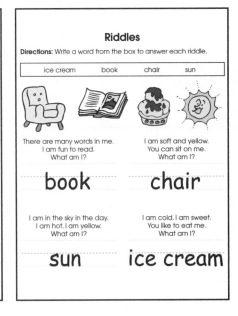

There are many words in me.
I am fun to read.
What am I?

book

I am soft and yellow.
You can sit on me.
What am I?

chair

I am in the sky in the day.
I am hot. I am yellow.
What am I?

sun

I am cold. I am sweet.
You like to eat me.
What am I?

ice cream

Page 68

Picture Clues

Directions: Read the sentence. Circle the word that makes sense. Use the picture clues to help you. Then write the word.

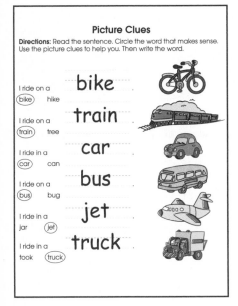

I ride on a
(bike) hike
bike

I ride on a
(train) tree
train

I ride in a
(car) can
car

I ride on a
(bus) bug
bus

I ride in a
jar (jet)
jet

I ride in a
took (truck)
truck

Page 69

Picture Clues

Directions: Read the sentence. Circle the word that makes sense. Use the picture clues to help you. Then write the word.

I see the
(bird) book
bird

I see the
(fish) fork
fish

I see the
(dogs) dig
dogs

I see the
(cats) coats
cats

I see the
(snake) snow
snake

I see the
(rat) rake
rat

Page 70

Comprehension

Directions: Look at the picture. Write the words from the box to finish the sentences.

| frog | log | bird | fish | ducks |

The **frog** can jump.

The turtle is on a **log**

A **bird** is in the tree.

The boy wants a **fish**.

I see three **ducks**

Page 71

Comprehension

Directions: Read the poem. Write the correct words in the blanks.

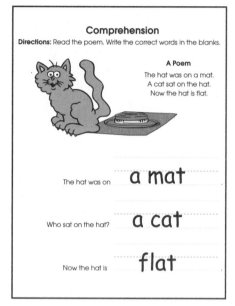

A Poem
The hat was on a mat.
A cat sat on the hat.
Now the hat is flat.

The hat was on   a mat

Who sat on the hat?   a cat

Now the hat is   flat

Page 72

Following Directions: Color the Path

Directions: Color the path the girl should take to go home. Use the sentences to help you.

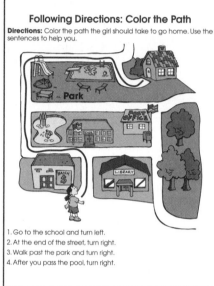

1. Go to the school and turn left.
2. At the end of the street, turn right.
3. Walk past the park and turn right.
4. After you pass the pool, turn right.

Page 73

Following Directions

Directions: Look at the pictures. Follow the directions in each box.

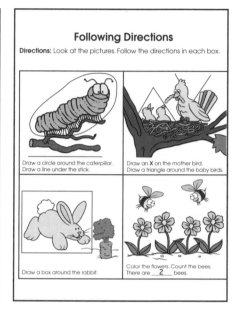

Page 74

Classifying

Directions: Classifying is sorting things into groups. Draw a circle around the pictures that answer the question.

What Can Swim?

What Can Fly?

Page 75

Classifying: These Keep Me Warm

Directions: Color the things that keep you warm.

Page 76

Classifying: Objects

Help Dan clean up the park.

Directions: Circle the litter. Underline the coins. Draw a box around the balls.

Page 77

Classifying: Things to Drink

Directions: Circle the pictures of things you can drink. Write the names of those things in the blanks.

milk
juice   soda

Page 78

Vocabulary

Directions: Read the words. Trace and write them on the lines. Look at each picture. Write **hot** or **cold** on the lines to show if it is hot or cold.

hot hot hot hot

cold cold cold

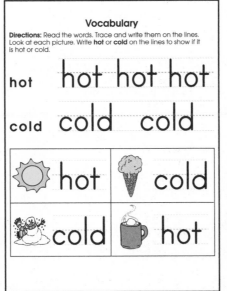

hot   cold

cold   hot

Page 79

Vocabulary

Directions: Read the words. Trace and write them on the lines. Look at each picture and write **day** or **night** on the lines to show if they happen during the day or night.

day day day

night night night

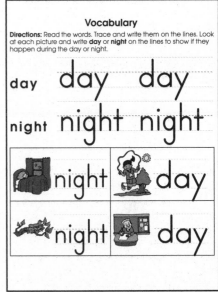

night   day

night   day

Page 80

Classifying: Night and Day

Directions: Write the words from the box under the pictures they describe.

stars sun moon rays dark light night day

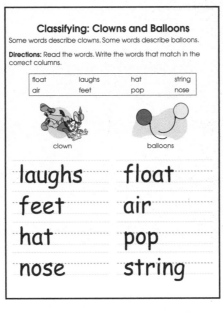

stars   sun
moon   rays
dark   light
night   day

Page 81

Classifying: Clowns and Balloons

Some words describe clowns. Some words describe balloons.

Directions: Read the words. Write the words that match in the correct columns.

| float | laughs | hat | string |
| air | feet | pop | nose |

clown   balloons

laughs   float
feet   air
hat   pop
nose   string

Page 82

Similarities: Objects

Directions: Circle the picture in each row that is most like the first picture.

Example:

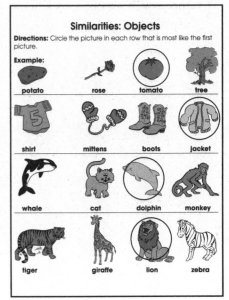

potato   rose   tomato   tree

shirt   mittens   boots   jacket

whale   cat   dolphin   monkey

tiger   giraffe   lion   zebra

Page 83

Similarities: Objects

Directions: Circle the picture in each row that is most like the first picture.

Example:

carrot — jacks — bread — (pea)

baseball — sneakers — (basketball) — bat

store — school — (home) — bakery

kitten — dog — fox — (cat)

Page 84

Classifying: Food Groups

Directions: Color the meats and eggs blue. Color the fruits and vegetables green. Color the breads tan. Color the dairy foods (milk and cheese) yellow.

fish — bread — apple — cheese

crackers — carrot — orange — eggs

steaks — pear — milk — yogurt

ice cream — chicken — potato — pretzel

Page 85

Same and Different: These Don't Belong

Directions: Circle the pictures in each row that go together.

Row 1 — cookies — cake — beans — ice cream

Row 2 — apple — banana — orange — cookies

Row 3 — kite — dice — checkers — chess

Directions: Write the names of the things that do not belong.

Row 1 — beans
Row 2 — cookies
Row 3 — kite

Page 86

Classifying: What Does Not Belong?

Directions: Draw an **X** on the picture that does not belong in each group.

fruit: apple — peach — corn (X) — watermelon

wild animals: bear — kitten (X) — gorilla — lion

pets: cat — fish — elephant (X) — dog

flowers: grass (X) — rose — daisy — tulip

Page 87

Classifying: What Does Not Belong?

Directions: Draw an **X** on the word in each row that does not belong.

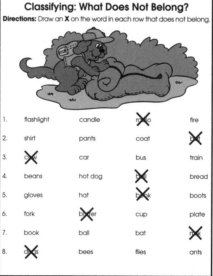

1. flashlight — candle — radio (X) — fire
2. shirt — pants — coat — bat (X)
3. city (X) — car — bus — train
4. beans — hot dog — ball (X) — bread
5. gloves — hat — book (X) — boots
6. fork — butter (X) — cup — plate
7. book — ball — bat — milk (X)
8. dogs (X) — bees — flies — ants

Page 88

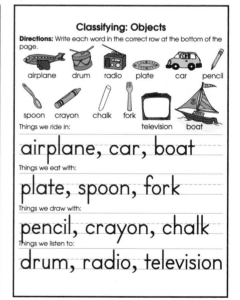

Classifying: Objects

Directions: Write each word in the correct row at the bottom of the page.

airplane — drum — radio — plate — car — pencil
spoon — crayon — chalk — fork — television — boat

Things we ride in:
airplane, car, boat

Things we eat with:
plate, spoon, fork

Things we draw with:
pencil, crayon, chalk

Things we listen to:
drum, radio, television

GRADE 1

Page 89

Classifying: Names, Numbers, Animals, Colors
Directions: Write the words from the box next to the words they describe.

Joe	cat	blue	Tim
two	dog	red	ten
Sue	green	pig	six

Name Words: Joe Tim Sue

Number Words: two ten six

Animal Words: cat dog pig

Color Words: green red blue

Page 90

Classifying: Things That Belong Together
Directions: Circle the pictures in each row that belong together.

Row 1 — knife, key, fork, spoon
Row 2 — orange, apple, candy, banana
Row 3 — beach ball, soccer ball, baseball, apple

Directions: Write the names of the pictures that do not belong.

Row 1: key
Row 2: candy
Row 3: apple

Page 91

Classifying: Why They Are Different
Directions: Look at your answers on page 90. Write why each object does not belong.

You don't eat with a key.
A candy is not a fruit.
An apple is not a ball.

Directions: For each object, draw a group of pictures that belong with it.

candy bar — Drawings will vary.

lettuce — Drawings will vary.

Page 92

Classifying: What Does Not Belong?
Directions: Circle the two things that do not belong in the picture. Write why they do not belong.

1. Flowers do not grow in snow.
2. Palm trees do not grow in snow.

Page 93

Sequencing: Fill the Glasses
Directions: Follow the instructions to fill each glass. Use crayons to draw your favorite drink in the ones that are full and half-full.

full, half-full, empty
empty, half-full, full

Page 94

Sequencing: Raking Leaves
Directions: Write a number in each box to show the order of the story.

1 4 3 2

Page 95

Sequencing: Make a Snowman!

Directions: Write the number of the sentence that goes with each picture in the box.

1. Roll a large snowball for the snowman's bottom.

2. Make another snowball and put it on top of the first.

3. Put the last snowball on top.

4. Dress the snowman.

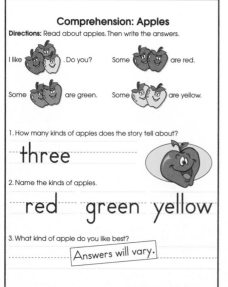

Page 96

Sequencing: A Recipe

Directions: Look at the recipe below. Put each step in order. Write **1, 2, 3** or **4** in the box.

HOW TO MAKE BREAD BUDDIES

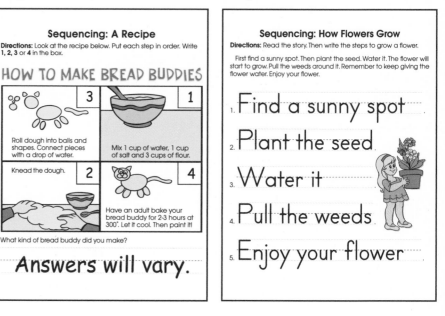

3	1
Roll dough into balls and shapes. Connect pieces with a drop of water.	Mix 1 cup of water, 1 cup of salt and 3 cups of flour.
Knead the dough. **2**	**4** Have an adult bake your bread buddy for 2-3 hours at 300°. Let it cool. Then paint it!

What kind of bread buddy did you make?

Answers will vary.

Page 97

Sequencing: How Flowers Grow

Directions: Read the story. Then write the steps to grow a flower.

First find a sunny spot. Then plant the seed. Water it. The flower will start to grow. Pull the weeds around it. Remember to keep giving the flower water. Enjoy your flower.

1. Find a sunny spot

2. Plant the seed

3. Water it

4. Pull the weeds

5. Enjoy your flower

Page 98

Comprehension: Apples

Directions: Read about apples. Then write the answers.

I like [apples]. Do you? Some [apples] are red.

Some [apples] are green. Some [apples] are yellow.

1. How many kinds of apples does the story tell about?

three

2. Name the kinds of apples.

red   green   yellow

3. What kind of apple do you like best?

Answers will vary.

Page 99

Comprehension: Crayons

Directions: Read about crayons. Then write your answers.

Crayons come in many colors. Some crayons are dark colors. Some crayons are light colors. All crayons have wax in them.

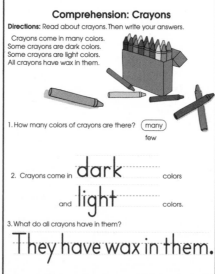

1. How many colors of crayons are there?   (many)   few

2. Crayons come in **dark** colors and **light** colors.

3. What do all crayons have in them?

They have wax in them.

Page 100

Comprehension

Directions: Read the story. Write the words from the story that complete each sentence.

Jane and Bill like to play in the rain. They take off their shoes and socks. They splash in the puddles. It feels cold! It is fun to splash!

Jane and Bill like to **play in the rain**

They take off their **shoes and socks**

They splash in **the puddles**

Do you like to splash in puddles?   (Yes)   No

Page 101

Comprehension

Directions: Read the story. Write the words from the story that complete each sentence.

Ben and Sue have a bug.
It is red with black spots.
They call it Spot.
Spot likes to eat green leaves and grass.
The children keep Spot in a box.

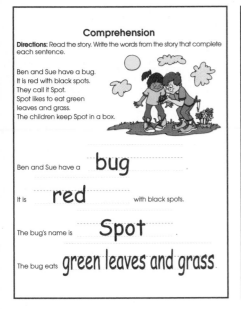

Ben and Sue have a __bug__

It is __red__ with black spots.

The bug's name is __Spot__

The bug eats __green leaves and grass__

Page 102

Comprehension: Growing Flowers

Directions: Read about flowers. Then write the answers.

Some flowers grow in pots. Many flowers grow in flower beds. Others grow beside the road. Flowers begin from seeds. They grow into small buds. Then they open wide and bloom. Flowers are pretty!

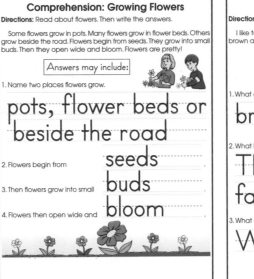

| Answers may include: |

1. Name two places flowers grow.

__pots, flower beds or beside the road__

2. Flowers begin from __seeds__

3. Then flowers grow into small __buds__

4. Flowers then open wide and __bloom__

Page 103

Comprehension: Raking Leaves

Directions: Read about raking leaves. Then answer the questions.

I like to rake leaves. Do you? Leaves die each year. They get brown and dry. They fall from the trees. Then we rake them up.

1. What color are leaves when they die?

__brown__

2. What happens when they die?

__They get dry and fall from the tree.__

3. What do we do when leaves fall?

__We rake them.__

Page 104

Comprehension: Clocks

Directions: Read about clocks. Then answer the questions.

Ticking Clocks

Many clocks make two sounds. The sounds are tick and tock. Big clocks often make loud tick-tocks. Little clocks often make quiet tick-tocks. Sometimes people put little clocks in a box with a new puppy. The puppy likes the sound. The tick-tock makes the puppy feel safe.

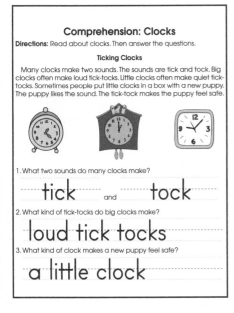

1. What two sounds do many clocks make?

__tick__ and __tock__

2. What kind of tick-tocks do big clocks make?

__loud tick tocks__

3. What kind of clock makes a new puppy feel safe?

__a little clock__

Page 105

Comprehension: Soup

Directions: Read about soup. Then write the answers.

I Like Soup

Soup is good! It is good for you, too. We eat most kinds of soup hot. Some people eat cold soup in the summer. Carrots and beans are in some soups. Do you like crackers with soup?

1. Name two ways people eat soup.

__cold__   __hot__

2. Name two things that are in some soups.

__carrots__   __beans__

3. Name the kind of soup you like best.

__Answers will vary.__

Page 106

Comprehension: The Teddy Bear Song

Do you know the Teddy Bear Song? It is very old!

Directions: Read the Teddy Bear Song. Then answer the questions.

Teddy bear, teddy bear, turn around.
Teddy bear, teddy bear, touch the ground.
Teddy bear, teddy bear, climb upstairs.
Teddy bear, teddy bear, say your prayers.
Teddy bear, teddy bear, turn out the light.
Teddy bear, teddy bear, say, "Good night!"

1. What is the first thing the teddy bear does?

__He turns around.__

2. What is the last thing the teddy bear does?

__He says, "Good night!"__

3. What would you name a teddy bear?

__Answers will vary.__

Page 107

Sequencing: Put Teddy Bear to Bed

Directions: Read the song about the teddy bear again. Write a number in each box to show the order of the story.

Page 108

Comprehension: A New Teddy Bear Song

Directions: Write words to make a new teddy bear song. Act out your new song with your teddy bear as you read it.

Answers will vary.

Teddy bear, teddy bear, turn

Teddy bear, teddy bear, touch the

Teddy bear, teddy bear, climb

Teddy bear, teddy bear, turn out

Teddy bear, teddy bear, say,

Page 109

Sequencing: Petting a Cat

Directions: Read the story. Then write the answers.

Do you like cats? I do. To pet a cat, move slowly. Hold out your hand. The cat will come to you. Then pet its head. Do not grab a cat! It will run away.

To pet a cat . . .

1. Move **slowly**

2. Hold out your **hand**

3. The cat will come to **you**

4. Pet the cat's **head**

5. Do not **grab** a cat!

Page 110

Comprehension: Cats

Directions: Read the story about cats again. Then write the answers.

1. What is a good title for the story?

Answers will vary.

2. The story tells you how to **pet a cat**

3. What part of your body should you pet a cat with?

your hand

4. Why should you move slowly to pet a cat?

Answers will vary.

5. Why do you think a cat will run away if you grab it?

Answers will vary.

Page 111

Comprehension: Cats

Directions: Look at the pictures and read about four cats. Then write the correct name beside each cat.

Fluffy, Blackie and Tiger are playing. Tom is sleeping. Blackie has spots. Tiger has stripes.

Fluffy

Tiger

Blackie

Tom

Page 112

Same and Different: Cats

Directions: Compare the picture of the cats on page 149 to this picture. Write a word from the box to tell what is different about each cat.

| purple ball | green bow | blue brush | red collar |

1. Tom is wearing a **red collar**

2. Blackie has a **blue brush**

3. Fluffy is wearing a **green bow**

4. Tiger has a **purple ball**

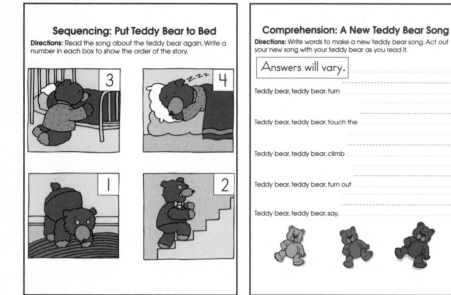
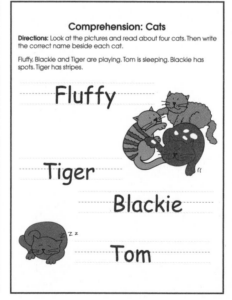
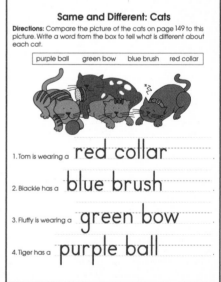

Page 113

Comprehension: Tigers

Directions: Read about tigers. Then write the answers.

Tigers sleep during the day. They hunt at night. Tigers eat meat. They hunt deer. They like to eat wild pigs. If they cannot find meat, tigers will eat fish.

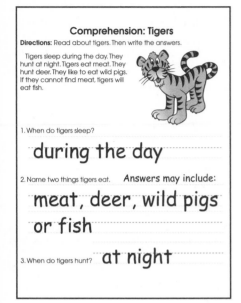

1. When do tigers sleep?

during the day

2. Name two things tigers eat.   **Answers may include:**

meat, deer, wild pigs or fish

3. When do tigers hunt?   **at night**

Page 114

Following Directions: Tiger Puzzle

Directions: Read the story about tigers again. Then complete the puzzle.

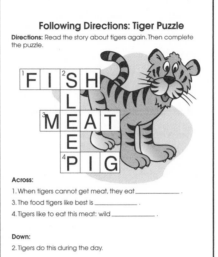

Crossword:
- ¹F I ²S H
- S L E E
- ³M E A T
- ⁴P I G

Across:

1. When tigers cannot get meat, they eat _____ .
3. The food tigers like best is _____ .
4. Tigers like to eat this meat: wild _____ .

Down:

2. Tigers do this during the day.

Page 115

Following Directions: Draw a Tiger

Directions: Follow directions to complete the picture of the tiger.

1. Draw black stripes on the tiger's body and tail.
2. Color the tiger's tongue red.
3. Draw claws on the feet.
4. Draw a black nose and two black eyes on the tiger's face.
5. Color the rest of the tiger orange.
6. Draw tall, green grass for the tiger to sleep in.

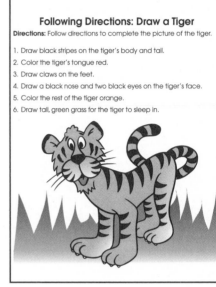

Page 116

Comprehension: Write a Party Invitation

Directions: Read about the party. Then complete the invitation.

The party will be at Dog's house. The party will start at 1:00 P.M. It will last 2 hours. Write your birthday for the date of the party.

Party Invitation

Where: **Dog's house**

Date: **Answers will vary.**

Time It Begins: **1:00** P.M.

Time It Ends: **3:00** P.M.

Answers will vary.

Directions: On the last line, write something else about the party.

Page 117

Sequencing: Pig Gets Ready

Directions: Number the pictures of Pig getting ready for the party to show the order of the story.

What kind of party do you think Pig is going to?   **Answers will vary.**

Page 118

Comprehension: An Animal Party

Directions: Use the picture for clues. Write words from the box to answer the questions.

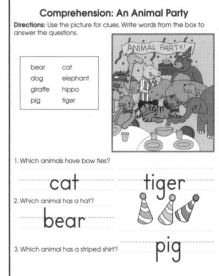

bear	cat
dog	elephant
giraffe	hippo
pig	tiger

1. Which animals have bow ties?

cat   **tiger**

2. Which animal has a hat?

bear

3. Which animal has a striped shirt?

pig

Page 119

Classifying: Party Items

Directions: Draw a ☐ around objects that are food for the party. Draw a △ around the party guests. Draw a ◯ around the objects used for fun at the party.

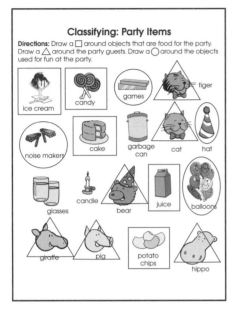

Page 120

Comprehension: Rhymes

Directions: Read about words that rhyme. Then circle the answers.

Words that rhyme have the same end sounds. "Wing" and "sing" rhyme. "Boy" and "toy" rhyme. "Dime" and "time" rhyme. Can you think of other words that rhyme?

1. Words that rhyme have the same ⟨end sounds.⟩ end letters.

2. "Time" rhymes with "tree." ⟨"dime."⟩

Directions: Write one rhyme for each word.

wing | Answers will vary. | boy

dime | | pink

Page 121

Rhyming Words

Many poems have rhyming words. The rhyming words are usually at the end of the line.

Directions: Complete the poem with words from the box.

My Glue

I spilled my **glue**

I felt **blue**

What could I **do** ?

Hey! I have a **clue** !

I'll make it **clean**

The cleanest you've **seen**

No one will **scream**

Wouldn't that be **mean** ?

blue	clue	scream	seen
glue	do	clean	mean

Page 122

Classifying: Rhymes

Directions: Circle the pictures in each row that rhyme.

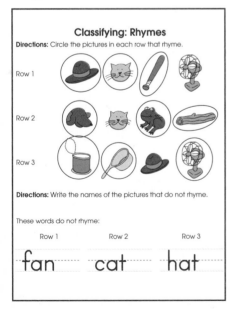

Row 1

Row 2

Row 3

Directions: Write the names of the pictures that do not rhyme.

These words do not rhyme:

Row 1 | Row 2 | Row 3

fan **cat** **hat**

Page 123

Predicting: Words and Pictures

Directions: Complete each story by choosing the correct picture. Draw a line from the story to the picture.

1. Shawnda got her books. She went to the bus stop. Shawnda got on the bus.

2. Marco planted a seed. He watered it. He pulled the weeds around it.

3. Abraham's dog was barking. Abraham got out the dog food. He put it in the dog bowl.

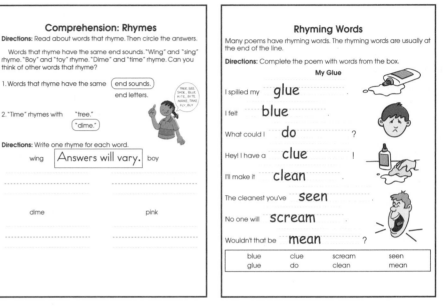

Page 124

Predicting: Story Ending

Directions: Read the story. Draw a picture in the last box to complete the story.

That's my ball. | I got it first.

1 | 2 | 3 | 4 Pictures will vary.

It's mine!

Total Basic Skills Grade 1

Page 125

Predicting: Story Ending

Directions: Read the story. Draw a picture in the last box to complete the story.

Marco likes to paint.   He likes to help his dad.

Pictures will vary.

He is tired when he's finished.

Page 126

Predicting: Story Ending

Directions: Read each story. Circle the sentence that tells how the story will end.

Ann was riding her bike. She saw a dog in the park. She stopped to pet it. Ann left to go home.

The dog went swimming.

(The dog followed Ann.)

The dog went home with a cat.

Antonio went to a baseball game. A baseball player hit a ball toward him. He reached out his hands.

The player caught the ball.

The ball bounced on a car.

(Antonio caught the ball.)

Page 127

Making Inferences: Baseball

Traci likes baseball. She likes to win. Traci's team does not win.

Directions: Circle the correct answers.

1. Traci likes

   football.   soccer.   (baseball.)

2. Traci likes to   (win.)   lose.

3. Traci uses a bat.   (Yes)   No

4. Traci is   happy.   (sad.)

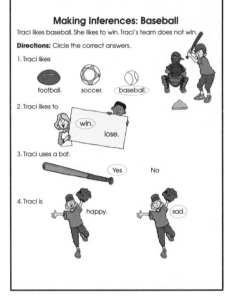

Page 128

Making Inferences: The Stars

Lynn looks at the stars. She sings a song about them. She makes a wish on them. The stars help Lynn sleep.

Directions: Circle the correct answers.

1. Lynn likes the

   moon.   sun.   (stars.)

2. What song do you think she sings?

   Row, Row, Row Your Boat

   (Twinkle, Twinkle Little Star)

   Happy Birthday to You

3. What does Lynn "make" on the stars?

   (a wish)   a spaceship   lunch

Page 129

Making Inferences: Feelings

Directions: Read each story. Choose a word from the box to show how each person feels.

happy	excited	sad	mad

1. Andy and Sam were best friends. Sam and his family moved far away. How does Sam feel?

   sad

2. Deana could not sleep. It was the night before her birthday party. How does Deana feel?

   excited

3. Jacob let his baby brother play with his teddy bear. His brother lost the bear. How does Jacob feel?

   mad

4. Kia picked flowers for her mom. Her mom smiled when she got them. How does Kia feel?

   happy

Page 130

Books

Directions: What do you know about books? Use the words in the box below to help fill in the lines.

title	book	author
illustrator	pages	left to right
fun	library	glossary

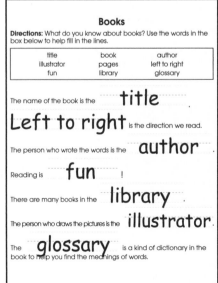

The name of the book is the **title**

Left to right is the direction we read.

The person who wrote the words is the **author**

Reading is **fun** !

There are many books in the **library** .

The person who draws the pictures is the **illustrator**.

The **glossary** is a kind of dictionary in the book to help you find the meanings of words.

Page 132

Nouns

A noun is a word that names a person, place or thing. When you read a sentence, the noun is what the sentence is about.

Directions: Complete each sentence with a noun.

The **cat** is fat.

My **house** is blue.

The **tree** has apples.

The **sun** is hot.

Page 133

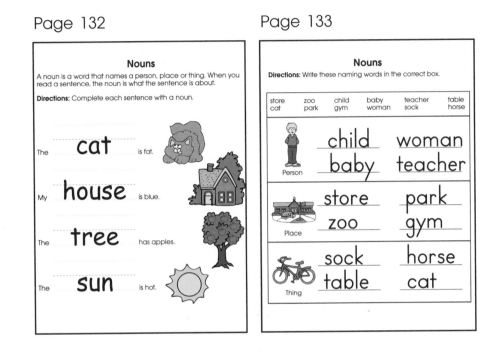

Nouns

Directions: Write these naming words in the correct box.

store	zoo	child	baby	teacher	table
cat	park	gym	woman	sock	horse

Person: child, woman, baby, teacher

Place: store, park, zoo, gym

Thing: sock, horse, table, cat

Page 134

Things That Go Together

Some nouns name things that go together.

Directions: Draw a line to match the nouns on the left with the things they go with on the right.

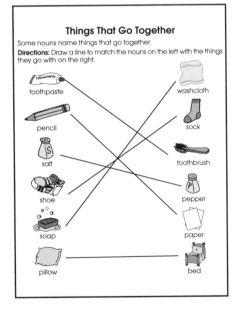

toothpaste — washcloth
pencil — sock
salt — toothbrush
shoe — pepper
soap — paper
pillow — bed

Page 135

Tracking: Things That Go Together

Directions: Draw a line to connect the objects that go together.

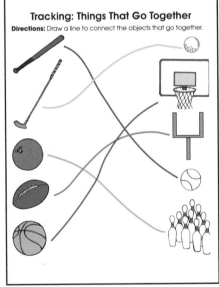

Page 136

Verbs

Verbs are words that tell what a person or a thing can do.

Example: The girl pats the dog.
The word **pats** is the verb. It shows action.

Directions: Draw a line between the verbs and the pictures that show the action.

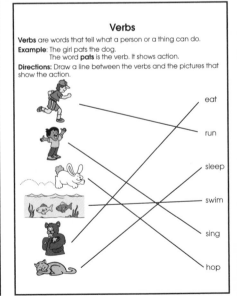

eat
run
sleep
swim
sing
hop

Page 137

Verbs

Directions: Look at the picture and read the words. Write an action word in each sentence below.

1. The two boys like to ___talk___ together.
2. The children ___kick___ the soccer ball.
3. Some children like to ___swing___ on the swing.
4. The girl can ___run___ very fast.
5. The teacher ___rings___ the bell.

Page 138

Words That Describe

Describing words tell us more about a person, place or thing.

Directions: Read the words in the box. Choose the word that describes the picture. Write it next to the picture.

| happy | round | sick | cold | long |

long
happy
sick
round
cold

Page 139

Words That Describe

Directions: Read the words in the box. Choose the word that describes the picture. Write it next to the picture.

| wet | round | funny | soft | sad | tall |

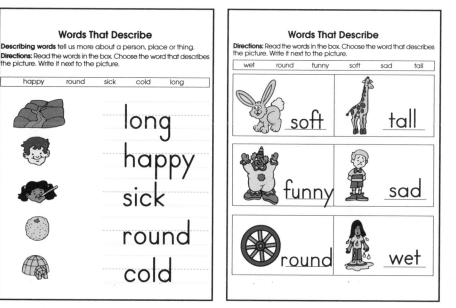

soft   tall
funny   sad
round   wet

Page 140

Words That Describe

Directions: Circle the describing word in each sentence. Draw a line from the sentence to the picture.

1. The hungry dog is eating.
2. The tiny bird is flying.
3. Horses have long legs.
4. She is a fast runner.
5. The little boy was lost.

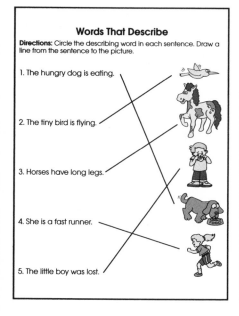

Page 141

Words That Describe: Colors and Numbers

Colors and numbers can describe nouns.

Directions: Underline the describing word in each sentence. Draw a picture to go with each sentence.

A yellow moon was in the sky.

Pictures will vary.

Two worms are on the road.

The tree had red apples.

The girl wore a blue dress.

Page 142

Sequencing: Comparative Adjectives

Directions: Look at each group of pictures. Write 1, 2 or 3 under the picture to show where it should be.

Example:

tallest ___3___   tall ___1___   taller ___2___

small ___1___   smallest ___3___   smaller ___2___

biggest ___3___   big ___1___   bigger ___2___

wider ___2___   wide ___1___   widest ___3___

Page 143

Sequencing: Comparative Adjectives

Directions: Look at the pictures in each row. Write 1, 2 or 3 under the picture to show where it should be.

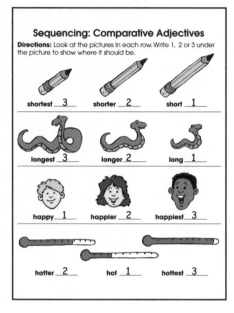

shortest _3_   shorter _2_   short _1_

longest _3_   longer _2_   long _1_

happy _1_   happier _2_   happiest _3_

hotter _2_   hot _1_   hottest _3_

Page 144

Synonyms

Synonyms are words that mean almost the same thing. **Start** and **begin** are synonyms.

Directions: Find the synonyms that describe each picture. Write the words in the boxes below the picture.

small funny large sad silly little big unhappy	
small	large
little	big
sad	silly
unhappy	funny

Page 145

Similarities: Synonyms

Directions: Circle the word in each row that is most like the first word in the row.

Example:

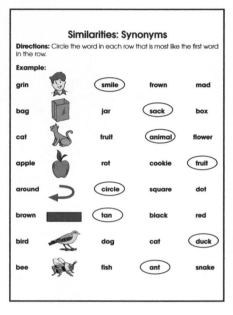

grin		**smile**	frown	mad
bag		jar	**sack**	box
cat		fruit	**animal**	flower
apple		rot	cookie	**fruit**
around		**circle**	square	dot
brown		**tan**	black	red
bird		dog	cat	**duck**
bee		fish	**ant**	snake

Page 146

Synonyms

Directions: Read each sentence and look at the underlined word. Circle the word that means the same thing. Write the new words.

1. The boy was <u>mad</u>.   happy   **angry**   pup
2. The <u>dog</u> is brown.   **pup**   cat   rat
3. I like to <u>scream</u>.   soar   mad   **shout**
4. The bird can <u>fly</u>.   **soar**   jog   warm
5. The girl can <u>run</u>.   sleep   **jog**   shout
6. I am <u>hot</u>.   **warm**   cold   soar

angry   **pup**   **shout**

soar   **jog**   **warm**

Page 147

Similarities: Synonyms

Directions: Read the story. Write a word on the line that means almost the same as the word under the line.

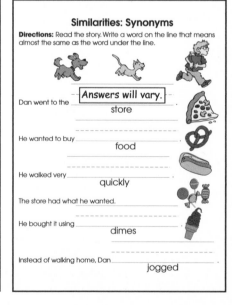

Answers will vary.

Dan went to the _____ store

He wanted to buy _____ food

He walked very _____ quickly

The store had what he wanted.

He bought it using _____ dimes

Instead of walking home, Dan _____ jogged

Page 148

Antonyms

Antonyms are words that are opposites. **Hot** and **cold** are antonyms.

Directions: Draw a line between the antonyms.

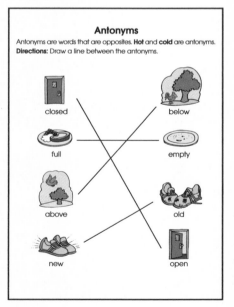

closed   below

full   empty

above   old

new   open

Page 149

Opposites

Directions: Draw lines to connect the words that are opposites.

up — wet
over — down
dry — dirty
clean — under

Page 150

Opposites

Opposites are things that are different in every way.

Directions: Draw a line between the opposites.

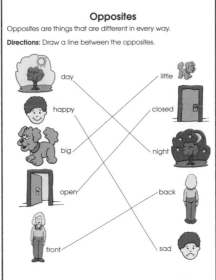

day — little
happy — closed
big — night
open — back
front — sad

Page 151

Opposites

Directions: Circle the picture in each row that is the opposite of the first picture.

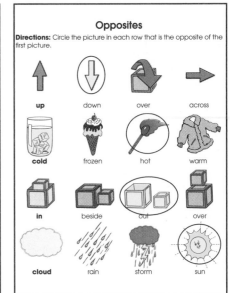

up — down — over — across
cold — frozen — hot — warm
in — beside — out — over
cloud — rain — storm — sun

Page 152

Opposites

Directions: Read each clue. Write the answers in the puzzle.

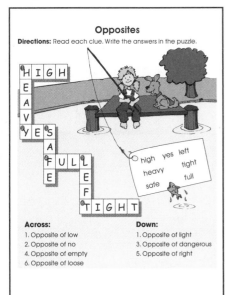

HIGH
HEAVY
YES
A
FULL
E   E
F
TIGHT

high   yes   left
heavy   tight
safe   full

Across:
1. Opposite of low
2. Opposite of no
4. Opposite of empty
6. Opposite of loose

Down:
1. Opposite of light
3. Opposite of dangerous
5. Opposite of right

Page 153

Homophones

Homophones are words that **sound** the same but are spelled differently and mean something different. **Blew** and **blue** are homophones.

Directions: Look at the word pairs. Choose the word that describes the picture. Write the word on the line next to the picture.

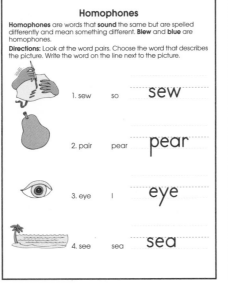

1. sew   so   sew

2. pair   pear   pear

3. eye   I   eye

4. see   sea   sea

Page 154

Homophones

Directions: Read each sentence. Underline the two words that sound the same but are spelled differently and mean something different.

1. Tom ate eight grapes.

2. Becky read Little Red Riding Hood.

3. I went to buy two dolls.

4. Five blue feathers blew in the wind.

5. Would you get wood for the fire?

Page 155

Sentences

Sentences begin with capital letters.

Directions: Read the sentences and write them below. Begin each sentence with a capital letter.

Example: the cat is fat.

The cat is fat.

my dog is big.

My dog is big.

the boy is sad.

The boy is sad.

bikes are fun!

Bikes are fun!

dad can bake.

Dad can bake.

Page 156

Word Order

If you change the order of the words in a sentence, you can change the meaning of the sentence.

Directions: Read the sentences. Draw a circle around the sentence that describes the picture.

Example:

The fox jumped over the dogs.
The dogs jumped over the fox.

1. The cat watched the bird.
   The bird watched the cat.

2. The girl looked at the boy.
   The boy looked at the girl.

3. The turtle ran past the rabbit.
   The rabbit ran past the turtle.

Page 157

Word Order

Directions: Look at the picture. Put the words in order. Write the sentences on the lines below.

1. We made lemonade. some
2. good. It was
3. We the sold lemonade.
4. cost It five cents.
5. fun. We had

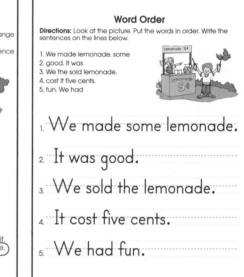

1. We made some lemonade.
2. It was good.
3. We sold the lemonade.
4. It cost five cents.
5. We had fun.

Page 158

Telling Sentences

Directions: Read the sentences and write them below. Begin each sentence with a capital letter. End each sentence with a period.

1. most children like pets
2. some children like dogs
3. some children like cats
4. some children like snakes
5. some children like all animals

1. Most children like pets.
2. Some children like dogs.
3. Some children like cats.
4. Some children like snakes.
5. Some children like all animals.

Page 159

Telling Sentences

Directions: Read the sentences and write them below. Begin each sentence with a capital letter. End each sentence with a period.

1. i like to go to the store with Mom
2. we go on Friday
3. i get to push the cart
4. i get to buy the cookies
5. i like to help Mom

1. I like to go to the store with Mom.
2. We go on Friday.
3. I get to push the cart.
4. I get to buy the cookies.
5. I like to help Mom.

Page 160

Asking Sentences

Directions: Write the first word of each asking sentence. Be sure to begin each question with a capital letter. End each question with a question mark.

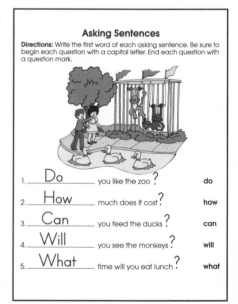

1. Do ____ you like the zoo? **do**
2. How ____ much does it cost? **how**
3. Can ____ you feed the ducks? **can**
4. Will ____ you see the monkeys? **will**
5. What ____ time will you eat lunch? **what**

Page 161

Asking Sentences

Directions: Read the asking sentences. Write the sentences below. Begin each sentence with a capital letter. End each sentence with a question mark.

1. what game will we play
2. do you like to read
3. how old are you
4. who is your best friend
5. can you tie your shoes

1. What game will we play?

2. Do you like to read?

3. How old are you?

4. Who is your best friend?

5. Can you tie your shoes?

Page 162

Periods and Question Marks

Directions: Put a period or a question mark at the end of each sentence below.

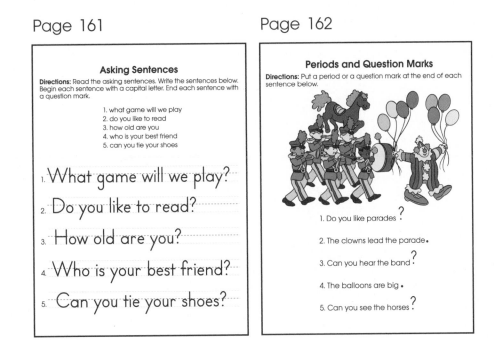

1. Do you like parades ?

2. The clowns lead the parade .

3. Can you hear the band ?

4. The balloons are big .

5. Can you see the horses ?

Page 163

Is and Are

We use **is** in sentences about one person or one thing. We use **are** in sentences about more than one person or thing.

Example: The dog **is** barking.
The dogs **are** barking.

Directions: Write **is** or **are** in the sentences below.

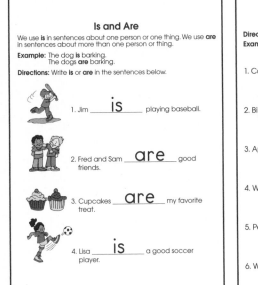

1. Jim _____is_____ playing baseball.

2. Fred and Sam _____are_____ good friends.

3. Cupcakes _____are_____ my favorite treat.

4. Lisa _____is_____ a good soccer player.

Page 164

Is and Are

Directions: Write **is** or **are** in the sentences below.
Example: Lisa _is_ sleeping.

1. Cats and dogs _are_ good pets.

2. Bill _is_ my best friend.

3. Apples _are_ good to eat.

4. We _are_ going to the zoo.

5. Pedro _is_ coming to my house.

6. When _are_ you all going to the zoo?

Page 166

Color Names

Directions: Trace the letters to write the name of each color. Then write the name again by yourself.

Example:

orange	orange
blue	blue
green	green
yellow	yellow
red	red
brown	brown

Page 167

Color Names: Sentences

Directions: Use the color words to complete these sentences. Then put a period at the end.

Example: My new [mittens] are **orange.**

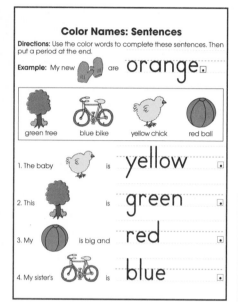

green tree   blue bike   yellow chick   red ball

1. The baby [chick] is **yellow.**

2. This [tree] is **green.**

3. My [ball] is big and **red.**

4. My sister's [bike] is **blue.**

Page 168

Animal Names

Directions: Fill in the missing letters for each word.

Example:

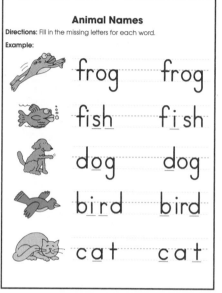

frog   frog

fish   fish

dog   dog

bird   bird

cat   cat

Page 169

Animal Names: Sentences

A **sentence** tells about something.

Directions: These sentences tell about animals. Write the word that completes each sentence.

Example:

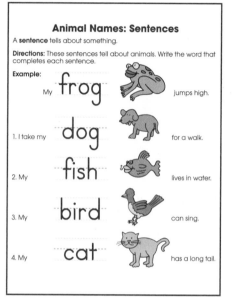

My **frog** jumps high.

1. I take my **dog** for a walk.

2. My **fish** lives in water.

3. My **bird** can sing.

4. My **cat** has a long tail.

Page 170

Things That Go

Directions: Trace the letters to write the name of each thing. Write each name again by yourself. Then color the pictures.

Example:

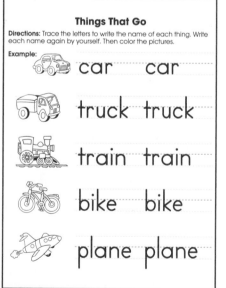

car   car

truck   truck

train   train

bike   bike

plane   plane

Page 171

Things That Go: Sentences

Directions: These sentences tell about things that go. Write the word that completes each sentence.

Example:

The **car** is in the garage.

1. The **truck** was at the farm.

2. My **bike** had a flat tire.

3. The **plane** flew high.

4. The **train** went fast.

Page 172

Clothing Words

Directions: Trace the letters to write the name of each clothing word. Then write each name again by yourself.

Example:

shirt   shirt

pants   pants

jacket   jacket

socks   socks

shoes   shoes

dress   dress

hat   hat

GRADE 1

Page 173

Clothing Words: Sentences

Directions: Some of these sentences tell a whole idea. Others have something missing. If something is missing, draw a line to the word that completes the sentence. Put a period at the end of each sentence.

Example:

She is wearing a polka-dot ————— holes .

1. The baseball player wore a

2. His pants were torn.

dress .

3. The socks had

4. The jacket had blue buttons.

hat .

5. The shoes were brown.

Page 174

Food Names

Directions: Trace the letters to write the name of each food word. Write each name again by yourself. Then color the pictures.

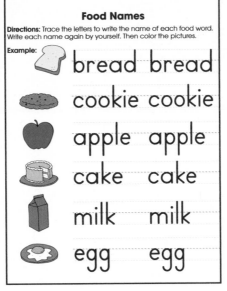

Example:

bread bread

cookie cookie

apple apple

cake cake

milk milk

egg egg

Page 175

Food Names: Asking Sentences

An **asking sentence** asks a question. Asking sentences end with a question mark.

Directions: Write each sentence on the line. Begin each sentence with a capital letter. Put a period at the end of the telling sentences and a question mark at the end of the asking sentences.

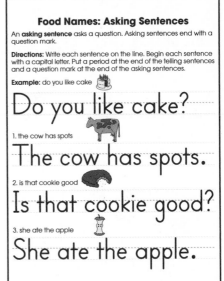

Example: do you like cake

Do you like cake?

1. the cow has spots

The cow has spots.

2. is that cookie good

Is that cookie good?

3. she ate the apple

She ate the apple.

Page 176

Number Words

Directions: Trace the letters to write the name of each number. Write the numbers again by yourself. Then color the number pictures.

Example:
Colors will vary.

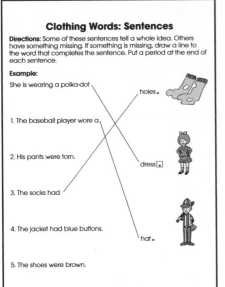

1 one one
2 two two
3 three three
4 four four
5 five five
6 six six
7 seven seven
8 eight eight
9 nine nine
10 ten ten

Page 177

Number Words: Asking Sentences

Directions: Use a number word to answer each question.

one	five	seven	three	eight

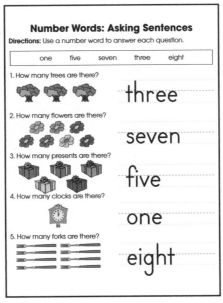

1. How many trees are there?

three

2. How many flowers are there?

seven

3. How many presents are there?

five

4. How many clocks are there?

one

5. How many forks are there?

eight

Page 178

Action Words

Action words tell things we can do.

Directions: Trace the letters to write each action word. Then write the action word again by yourself.

Example:

sleep sleep

run run

make make

ride ride

play play

stop stop

Page 179

Action Words: More Than One

To show more than one of something, add **s** to the end of the word.

Example: one cat   two cats

Directions: In each sentence, add **s** to show more than one. Then write the action word that completes each sentence.

sit	jump	stop	ride

Example:

The frog **s** **sleep** in the sun.

1. The boy **s** **sit** on the fence.

2. The car **s** **stop** at the sign.

3. The girl **s** **swim** in the water.

4. The dog **s** **sit** in the wagon.

Page 180

Action Words: Asking Sentences

Directions: Write an asking sentence about each picture. Begin each sentence with **can**. Add an action word. Begin each asking sentence with a capital letter and end it with a question mark.

Example:
I with you can

Can I sit with you?

she can

Can she cook?

with you can I

Can I play with you?

can she fast

Can she run fast?

Page 181

Sense Words

Directions: Circle the word that is spelled correctly. Then write the correct spelling in the blank.

Example: tast
(taste)   **taste**
tste

(touch)   **touch**
tuch
touh

smel
smll   **smell**
(smell)

her
(hear)   **hear**
har

(see)   **see**
se
sea

Page 182

Sense Words: Sentences

Directions: Read each sentence and write the correct words in the blanks.

Example:
taste
mouth   I can **taste** things with my **mouth**.

touch
hands   1. I can **touch** things with my **hands**.

nose
smell   2. I can **smell** things with my **nose**.

hear
ears   3. I can **hear** with my **ears**.

see
eyes   4. I can **see** things with my **eyes**.

Page 183

Weather Words: Beginning Sounds

Directions: Say the sound of the letter at the beginning of each row. Find the pictures in each row that begin with the same letter. Write the letter under the pictures.

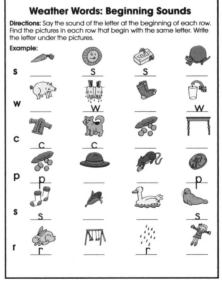

Example:

s   s   s

w   w   w

c   c   c

p   p   p

s   s   s

r   r   r

Page 184

Weather Words: Sentences

Directions: Write the weather word that completes each sentence. Put a period at the end of the telling sentences and a question mark at the end of the asking sentences.

Example:
Do flowers grow in the **sun** **?**

rain	water	wet	hot

1. The sun makes me **hot** **.**

2. When it rains, the grass gets **wet** **.**

3. Do you think it will **rain** on our picnic **?**

4. Should you drink the **water** from the rain **?**

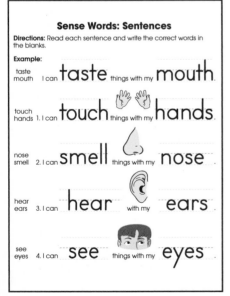

Page 185

My World

Directions: Fill in the missing letters for each word.

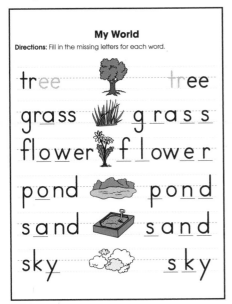

tr__ee__   tree

gr__ass__   gr__ass__

fl__owe__r   f__l__ow__e__r

p__o__nd   p__o__nd

s__a__nd   s__a__nd

sk__y__   sk__y__

Page 186

My World

Directions: The letters in the words below are mixed up. Unscramble the letters and write each word correctly.

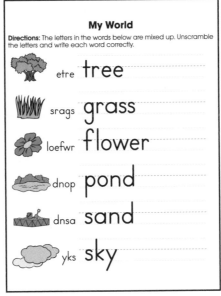

etre   tree

srags   grass

loefwr   flower

dnop   pond

dnsa   sand

yks   sky

Page 187

My World: Sentences

Directions: Write the word that completes each sentence. Put a period at the end of the telling sentences and a question mark at the end of the asking sentences.

Example: Does the sun shine on the __flowers__?

| tree | grass | pond | sand | sky |

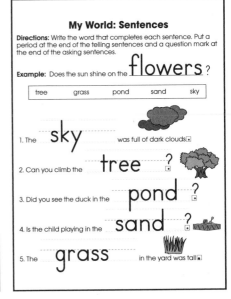

1. The __sky__ was full of dark clouds.

2. Can you climb the __tree__?

3. Did you see the duck in the __pond__?

4. Is the child playing in the __sand__?

5. The __grass__ in the yard was tall.

Page 188

The Parts of My Body: Sentences

Directions: Put a period at the end of the telling sentences and a question mark at the end of the asking sentences.

Example: I wear my hat on my __head__.

| arms | legs | feet | hands |

1. How strong are your __arms__?

2. You wear shoes on your __feet__.

3. If you're happy and you know it, clap your __hands__.

4. My pants covered my __legs__.

Page 189

The Parts of My Body: Sentences

Directions: Read the sentence parts below. Draw a line from the first part of the sentence to the second part that completes it.

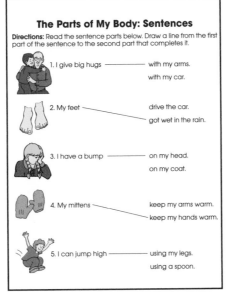

1. I give big hugs — with my arms.
   with my car.

2. My feet — drive the car.
   got wet in the rain.

3. I have a bump — on my head.
   on my coat.

4. My mittens — keep my arms warm.
   keep my hands warm.

5. I can jump high — using my legs.
   using a spoon.

Page 190

The Parts of My Body: Sentences

Directions: Read the two sentences on each line and draw a line between them. Then write each sentence again on the lines below. Begin each sentence with a capital letter, and end each one with a period or a question mark.

Example: wash your hands|they are dirty

Wash your hands.

They are dirty.

1. you have big arms|are you very strong

You have big arms.

Are you very strong?

2. I have two feet|I can run fast

I have two feet.

I can run fast.

Page 192

Number Recognition
Directions: Write the numbers 1-10. Color the bear.

1 2 3 4 5 6 7 8 9 10

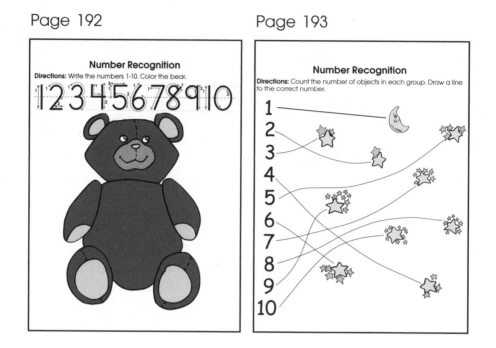

Page 193

Number Recognition
Directions: Count the number of objects in each group. Draw a line to the correct number.

1
2
3
4
5
6
7
8
9
10

Page 194

Counting
Directions: How many are there of each shape? Write the answers in the boxes. The first one is done for you.

☀ 1	☁ 7	🐦 6
🎈 10	🦔 3	🦒 2

Page 195

Counting
Directions: How many are there of each picture? Write the answers in the boxes. The first one is done for you.

☁ 7
🐸 4
🍎 10
🍂 5
🐦 3

Page 196

Number Word Find
Directions: Find the number words 0 through 12 hidden in the box.

```
t  e  a  z  w  z  x  a  b  i  g  t  e  n
o  l  z  r  b  e  r  e  v  e  d  l  a  j
t  w  e  l  v  e  a  b  o  n  e  c  d  z
i  a  r  p  q  d  p  s  k  e  q  u  i  w
c  f  f  p  l  a  s  k  i  q  u  e  h  o
m  s  t  f  v  u  k  e  z  t  u  f  i  d
t  n  u  w  s  i  x  f  w  h  g  h  g  o
a  s  g  c  g  d  f  o  u  r  j  m  r  f
a  s  g  c  o  f  c  o  h  h  p  o  m  i
n  y  c  q  b  s  o  k  n  o  w  v  p  v
b  e  x  v  s  s  e  v  e  n  m  e  n  e
t  h  r  e  e  r  t  a  l  j  k  a  q  z
m  o  a  n  e  n  i  m  u  t  w  a  y  y
```

Words to find:

zero	four	eight	eleven
one	five	nine	twelve
two	six	ten	
three	seven		

Page 197

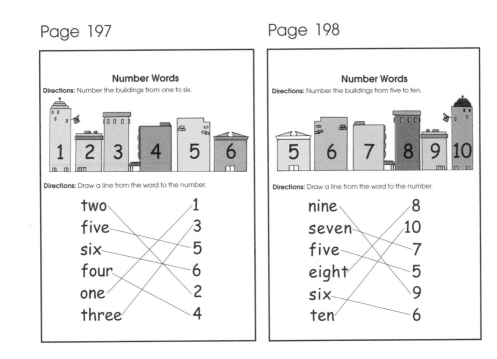

Page 198

Number Words
Directions: Number the buildings from one to six.

`1 2 3 4 5 6`

Directions: Draw a line from the word to the number.

two — 1
five — 3
six — 5
four — 6
one — 2
three — 4

Number Words
Directions: Number the buildings from five to ten.

`5 6 7 8 9 10`

Directions: Draw a line from the word to the number.

nine — 8
seven — 10
five — 7
eight — 5
six — 9
ten — 6

Page 199

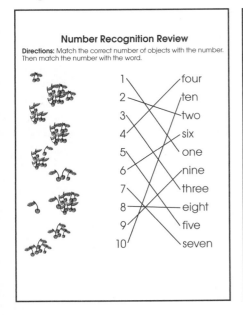

Number Recognition Review
Directions: Match the correct number of objects with the number. Then match the number with the word.

1 — four
2 — ten
3 — two
4 — six
5 — one
6 — nine
7 — three
8 — eight
9 — five
10 — seven

Page 200

Sequencing Numbers
Sequencing is putting numbers in the correct order.
1, 2, 3, 4, 5, 6, 7, 8, 9, 10
Directions: Write the missing numbers.

Example: 4, **5**, 6

3, **4**, 5   7, **8**, 9   8, **9**, 10
6, **7**, 8   **2**, 3, 4   **4**, 5, 6
5, 6, **7**   **5**, 6, 7   **2**, 3, 4
3, 4, 5   **6**, 7, 8   5, **6**, 7
2, 3, **4**   1, 2, **3**   7, 8, **9**
2, **3**, 4   **1**, 2, 3   4, **5**, 6
6, 7, **8**   3, 4, **5**   1, **2**, 3
7, 8, **9**   **2**, 3, 4   **8**, 9, 10

Page 201

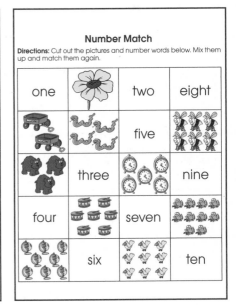

Number Match
Directions: Cut out the pictures and number words below. Mix them up and match them again.

one		two	eight
		five	
	three		nine
four		seven	
	six		ten

Page 203

Number Crossword Puzzle

Directions: Write the correct number word in the boxes provided.

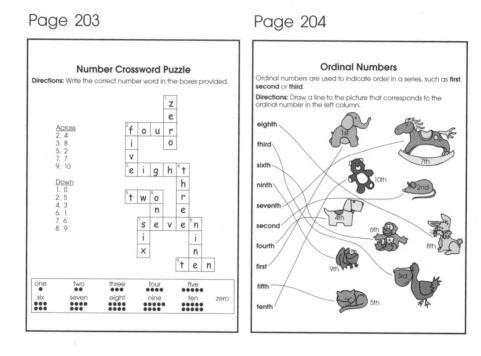

Across
2. 4
3. 8
5. 2
7. 7
9. 10

Down
1. 0
2. 5
4. 3
6. 1
7. 6
8. 9

| one ● | two ●● | three ●●● | four ●●●● | five ●●●●● |
| six ●●●●●● | seven ●●●●●●● | eight ●●●●●●●● | nine ●●●●●●●●● | ten ●●●●●●●●●● zero |

Page 204

Ordinal Numbers

Ordinal numbers are used to indicate order in a series, such as **first**, **second** or **third**.

Directions: Draw a line to the picture that corresponds to the ordinal number in the left column.

eighth
third
sixth
ninth
seventh
second
fourth
first
fifth
tenth

Page 205

Ordinal Numbers

Directions: Draw an **X** on the first vegetable, draw a circle around the second vegetable, and draw a square around the third vegetable.

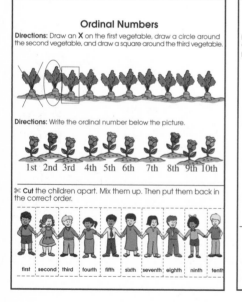

Directions: Write the ordinal number below the picture.

1st 2nd 3rd 4th 5th 6th 7th 8th 9th 10th

✂ **Cut** the children apart. Mix them up. Then put them back in the correct order.

first second third fourth fifth sixth seventh eighth ninth tenth

Page 207

Sequencing: At the Movies

Directions: The children are watching a movie. Read the sentences. Cut out the pictures below. Glue them where they belong in the picture.

1. The first child is eating popcorn.
2. The third child is eating candy.
3. The fourth child has a cup of fruit punch.
4. The second child is eating a big pretzel.

Page 209

Sequencing: Standing in Line

Directions: These children are waiting to see a movie. Look at them and follow the instructions.

1. Color the person who is first in line yellow.
2. Color the person who is last in line brown.
3. Color the person who is second in line pink.
4. Circle the person who is at the end of the line.

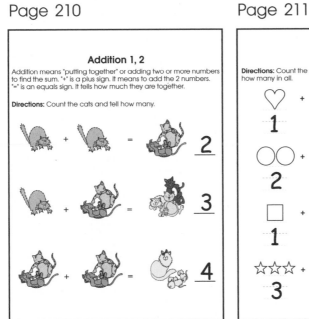

Page 210

Addition 1, 2

Addition means "putting together" or adding two or more numbers to find the sum. "+" is a plus sign. It means to add the 2 numbers. "=" is an equals sign. It tells how much they are together.

Directions: Count the cats and tell how many.

$+$ $=$ **2**

$+$ $=$ **3**

$+$ $=$ **4**

Page 211

Addition

Directions: Count the shapes and write the numbers below to tell how many in all.

♡ + ♡ = ♡♡
1   1   2

○○ + ○ = ○○○
2   1   3

□ + □□ = □□□
1   2   3

☆☆☆ + ☆ = ☆☆☆☆
3   1   4

Page 212

Addition

Directions: Draw the correct number of dots next to the numbers in each problem. Add up the number of dots to find your answer.

Example:

$\begin{array}{r} 3 \\ +2 \\ \hline 5 \end{array}$ $2 + 2 = \underline{4}$

$\begin{array}{r} 4 \\ +2 \\ \hline 6 \end{array}$ $1 + 5 = \underline{6}$

$\begin{array}{r} 3 \\ +1 \\ \hline 4 \end{array}$ $4 + 3 = \underline{7}$

$\begin{array}{r} 6 \\ +2 \\ \hline 8 \end{array}$ $5 + 3 = \underline{8}$

Page 213

Addition 3, 4, 5, 6

Directions: Practice writing the numbers and then add. Draw dots to help, if needed.

3 3 3 3   2   1
4 4 4 4   +4   +4
5 5 5 5 $\overline{6}$ $\overline{5}$
6 6 6 6   3   1
        +2   +2
        $\overline{5}$ $\overline{3}$

Page 214

Addition 4, 5, 6, 7

Directions: Practice writing the numbers and then add. Draw dots to help, if needed.

4 4 4 4   2   3
5 5 5 5   +5   +1
6 6 6 6 $\overline{7}$ $\overline{4}$
7 7 7 7   4   2
        +1   +4
        $\overline{5}$ $\overline{6}$

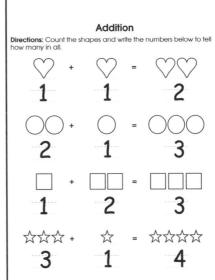

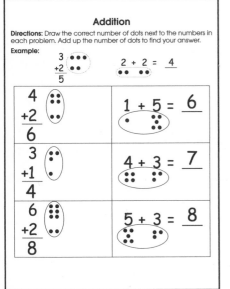

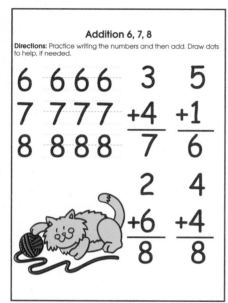
Page 215

Addition 6, 7, 8

Directions: Practice writing the numbers and then add. Draw dots to help, if needed.

6 6 6 6

7 7 7 7

8 8 8 8

$$\begin{array}{r} 3 \\ +4 \\ \hline 7 \end{array} \quad \begin{array}{r} 5 \\ +1 \\ \hline 6 \end{array}$$

$$\begin{array}{r} 2 \\ +6 \\ \hline 8 \end{array} \quad \begin{array}{r} 4 \\ +4 \\ \hline 8 \end{array}$$

Page 216

Addition 7, 8, 9

Directions: Practice writing the numbers and then add. Draw dots to help, if needed.

7 7 7 7

8 8 8 8

9 9 9 9

$$\begin{array}{r} 8 \\ +1 \\ \hline 9 \end{array} \quad \begin{array}{r} 3 \\ +5 \\ \hline 8 \end{array}$$

$$\begin{array}{r} 2 \\ +7 \\ \hline 9 \end{array} \quad \begin{array}{r} 6 \\ +1 \\ \hline 7 \end{array}$$

Page 217

Addition Table

Directions: Add across and down with a friend. Fill in the spaces.

+	0	1	2	3	4	5
0	0	1	2	3	4	5
1	1	2	3	4	5	6
2	2	3	4	5	6	7
3	3	4	5	6	7	8
4	4	5	6	7	8	9
5	5	6	7	8	9	10

Do you notice any number patterns in the Addition Table?

Page 218

Subtraction 1, 2, 3

Subtraction means "taking away" or subtracting one number from another. "−" is a minus sign. It means to subtract the second number from the first.
Directions: Practice writing the numbers and then subtract. Draw dots and cross them out, if needed.

1 1 1 1

2 2 2 2

3 3 3 3

$$\begin{array}{r} 3 \\ -1 \\ \hline 2 \end{array} \quad \begin{array}{r} 4 \\ -3 \\ \hline 1 \end{array}$$

$$\begin{array}{r} 2 \\ -1 \\ \hline 1 \end{array} \quad \begin{array}{r} 3 \\ -2 \\ \hline 1 \end{array}$$

Page 219

Subtraction 3, 4, 5, 6

Directions: Practice writing the numbers and then subtract. Draw dots and cross them out, if needed.

3 3 3 3

4 4 4 4

5 5 5 5

6 6 6 6

$$\begin{array}{r} 5 \\ -2 \\ \hline 3 \end{array} \quad \begin{array}{r} 6 \\ -1 \\ \hline 5 \end{array}$$

$$\begin{array}{r} 6 \\ -3 \\ \hline 3 \end{array} \quad \begin{array}{r} 5 \\ -1 \\ \hline 4 \end{array}$$

Page 220

Subtraction

Directions: Draw the correct number of dots next to the numbers in each problem. Cross out the ones subtracted to find your answer.

Example:

$$\begin{array}{r} 5 \\ -2 \\ \hline 3 \end{array} \quad 2 - 1 = 1$$

$\begin{array}{r} 4 - 2 = 2 \end{array}$	$\begin{array}{r} 8 \\ -6 \\ \hline 2 \end{array}$
$\begin{array}{r} 6 \\ -1 \\ \hline 5 \end{array}$	$3 - 1 = 2$
$9 - 6 = 3$	$\begin{array}{r} 4 \\ -3 \\ \hline 1 \end{array}$

Page 221

Review

Directions: Trace the numbers. Work the problems.

1 2 3 4 5 6 7 8 9 10

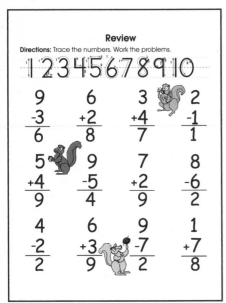

9 -3 6	6 +2 8	3 +4 7	2 -1 1
5 +4 9	9 -5 4	7 +2 9	8 -6 2
4 -2 2	6 +3 9	9 -7 2	1 +7 8

Page 222

Zero

Directions: Write the number.

Example:

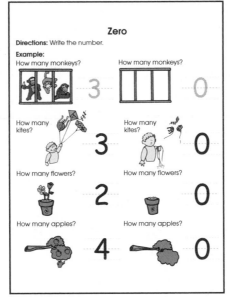

How many monkeys? 3   How many monkeys? 0

How many kites? 3   How many kites? 0

How many flowers? 2   How many flowers? 0

How many apples? 4   How many apples? 0

Page 223

Zero

Directions: Write the number that tells how many.

How many sailboats? 2   How many sailboats? 0

How many eggs? 6   How many eggs? 0

How many marshmallows? 4   How many marshmallows? 0

How many candles? 3   How many candles? 0

Page 224

Picture Problems: Addition

Directions: Solve the number problem under each picture.

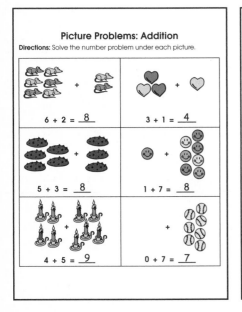

6 + 2 = 8   3 + 1 = 4

5 + 3 = 8   1 + 7 = 8

4 + 5 = 9   0 + 7 = 7

Page 225

Picture Problems: Addition

Directions: Solve the number problem under each picture.

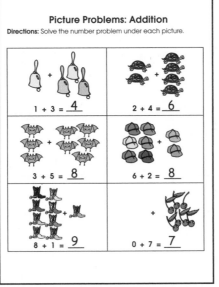

1 + 3 = 4   2 + 4 = 6

3 + 5 = 8   6 + 2 = 8

8 + 1 = 9   0 + 7 = 7

Page 226

Picture Problems: Subtraction

Directions: Solve the number problem under each picture.

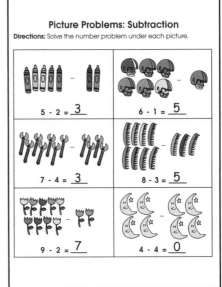

5 - 2 = 3   6 - 1 = 5

7 - 4 = 3   8 - 3 = 5

9 - 2 = 7   4 - 4 = 0

Page 227

Picture Problems: Subtraction

Directions: Solve the number problem under each picture.

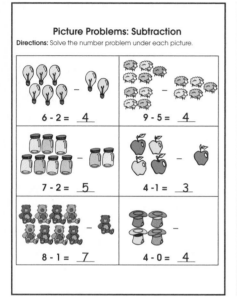

6 - 2 = __4__

9 - 5 = __4__

7 - 2 = __5__

4 - 1 = __3__

8 - 1 = __7__

4 - 0 = __4__

Page 228

Picture Problems: Addition and Subtraction

Directions: Solve the number problem under each picture.

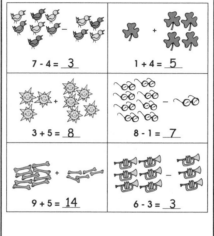

7 - 4 = __3__

1 + 4 = __5__

3 + 5 = __8__

8 - 1 = __7__

9 + 5 = __14__

6 - 3 = __3__

Page 229

Picture Problems: Addition and Subtraction

Directions: Solve the number problem under each picture. Write + or – to show if you should add or subtract.

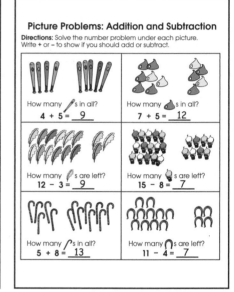

How many 🔪s in all?
4 + 5 = __9__

How many 👖s in all?
7 + 5 = __12__

How many 🖊s are left?
12 – 3 = __9__

How many 🐦s are left?
15 – 8 = __7__

How many 🍬s in all?
5 + 8 = __13__

How many ∩s are left?
11 – 4 = __7__

Page 230

Picture Problems: Addition and Subtraction

Directions: Solve the number problem under each picture. Write + or – to show if you should add or subtract.

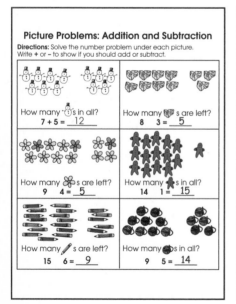

How many ☃s in all?
7 + 5 = __12__

How many 💗s are left?
8 3 = __5__

How many 🌼s are left?
9 4 = __5__

How many 🧍s in all?
14 1 = __15__

How many ✏s are left?
15 6 = __9__

How many 🐞s in all?
9 5 = __14__

Page 231

Review: Addition and Subtraction

Directions: Solve the number problem under each picture. Write + or – to show if you should add or subtract.

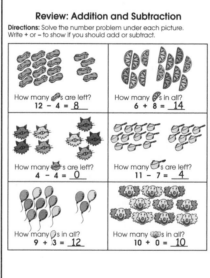

How many 🥜s are left?
12 – 4 = __8__

How many 🍊s in all?
6 + 8 = __14__

How many 🐱s are left?
4 – 4 = __0__

How many 🎻s are left?
11 – 7 = __4__

How many 🎈s in all?
9 + 3 = __12__

How many 🐑s in all?
10 + 0 = __10__

Page 232

Addition 1-5

Directions: Count the tools in each tool box. Write your answers in the blanks. Circle the problem that matches your answer.

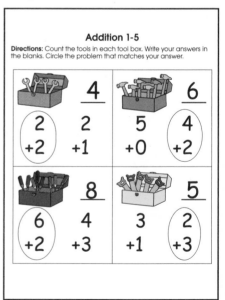

__4__

2   2
+2   +1

__6__

5   ④
+0   +2

__8__

⑥   4
+2   +3

__5__

3   ②
+1   +3

Page 233

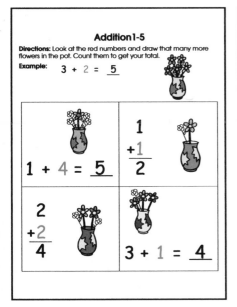

Addition 1-5

Directions: Look at the red numbers and draw that many more flowers in the pot. Count them to get your total.

Example: $3 + 2 = \underline{5}$

$1 + 4 = \underline{5}$

$\begin{array}{r} 1 \\ +1 \\ \hline 2 \end{array}$

$\begin{array}{r} 2 \\ +2 \\ \hline 4 \end{array}$

$3 + 1 = \underline{4}$

Page 234

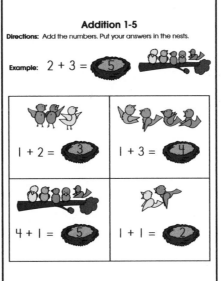

Addition 1-5

Directions: Add the numbers. Put your answers in the nests.

Example: $2 + 3 = \underline{5}$

$1 + 2 = \underline{3}$

$1 + 3 = \underline{4}$

$4 + 1 = \underline{5}$

$1 + 1 = \underline{2}$

Page 235

Addition 6-10

Directions: Add the numbers. Put your answers in the doghouses.

Example: $4 + 2 = \underline{6}$

$2 + 6 = \underline{8}$

$7 + 3 = \underline{10}$

$6 + 1 = \underline{7}$

$4 + 5 = \underline{9}$

$6 + 2 = \underline{8}$

$7 + 2 = \underline{9}$

Page 236

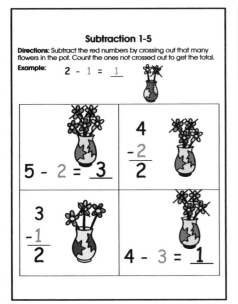

Subtraction 1-5

Directions: Subtract the red numbers by crossing out that many flowers in the pot. Count the ones not crossed out to get the total.

Example: $2 - 1 = \underline{1}$

$5 - 2 = \underline{3}$

$\begin{array}{r} 4 \\ -2 \\ \hline 2 \end{array}$

$\begin{array}{r} 3 \\ -1 \\ \hline 2 \end{array}$

$4 - 3 = \underline{1}$

Page 237

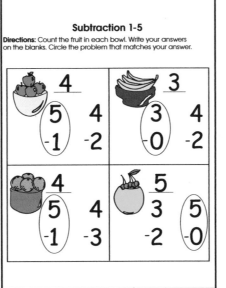

Subtraction 1-5

Directions: Count the fruit in each bowl. Write your answers on the blanks. Circle the problem that matches your answer.

$\begin{array}{r} 4 \\ \hline \end{array}$
$\begin{array}{r} 5 \\ -1 \end{array}$ (circled) $\quad \begin{array}{r} 4 \\ -2 \end{array}$

$\begin{array}{r} 3 \\ \hline \end{array}$
$\begin{array}{r} 3 \\ -0 \end{array}$ (circled) $\quad \begin{array}{r} 4 \\ -2 \end{array}$

$\begin{array}{r} 4 \\ \hline \end{array}$
$\begin{array}{r} 5 \\ -1 \end{array}$ (circled) $\quad \begin{array}{r} 4 \\ -3 \end{array}$

$\begin{array}{r} 5 \\ \hline \end{array}$
$\begin{array}{r} 3 \\ -2 \end{array} \quad \begin{array}{r} 5 \\ -0 \end{array}$ (circled)

Page 238

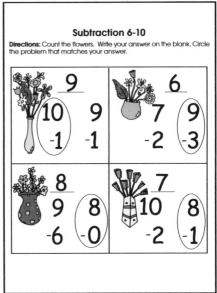

Subtraction 6-10

Directions: Count the flowers. Write your answer on the blank. Circle the problem that matches your answer.

$\begin{array}{r} 9 \\ \hline \end{array}$
$\begin{array}{r} 10 \\ -1 \end{array}$ (circled) $\quad \begin{array}{r} 9 \\ -1 \end{array}$

$\begin{array}{r} 6 \\ \hline \end{array}$
$\begin{array}{r} 7 \\ -2 \end{array} \quad \begin{array}{r} 9 \\ -3 \end{array}$ (circled)

$\begin{array}{r} 8 \\ \hline \end{array}$
$\begin{array}{r} 9 \\ -6 \end{array} \quad \begin{array}{r} 8 \\ -0 \end{array}$ (circled)

$\begin{array}{r} 7 \\ \hline \end{array}$
$\begin{array}{r} 10 \\ -2 \end{array} \quad \begin{array}{r} 8 \\ -1 \end{array}$ (circled)

Page 239

Addition and Subtraction

Directions: Solve the problems. Remember, addition means "putting together" or adding two or more numbers to find the sum. Subtraction means "taking away" or subtracting one number from another.

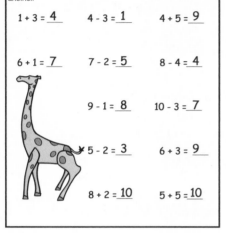

1 + 3 = 4   4 - 3 = 1   4 + 5 = 9

6 + 1 = 7   7 - 2 = 5   8 - 4 = 4

9 - 1 = 8   10 - 3 = 7

5 - 2 = 3   6 + 3 = 9

8 + 2 = 10   5 + 5 = 10

Page 240

Addition and Subtraction

Remember, addition means "putting together" or adding two or more numbers to find the sum. Subtraction means "take away" or subtracting one number from another.

Directions: Solve the problems. From your answers, use the code to color the quilt.

Color:
6 = blue
7 = yellow
8 = green
9 = red
10 = orange

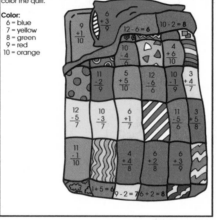

Page 241

Place Value: Tens and Ones

The place value of a digit, or numeral, is shown by where it is in the number. For example, in the number **23**, **2** has the place value of **tens**, and **3** is ones.

Directions: Count the groups of ten crayons and write the number by the word **tens**. Count the other crayons and write the number by the word **ones**.

Example: + = 1 ten + 1 one

= 2 tens + 3 ones

= 4 tens + 8 ones

= 7 tens + 2 ones

6 tens + 3 ones = 63   5 tens + 1 one = 51

3 tens + 8 ones = 38   9 tens + 7 ones = 97

4 tens + 5 ones = 45   2 tens + 8 ones = 28

Page 242

Place Value: Tens and Ones

Directions: Count the groups of ten blocks and write the number by the word tens. Count the other blocks and write the number by the word ones.

Example:

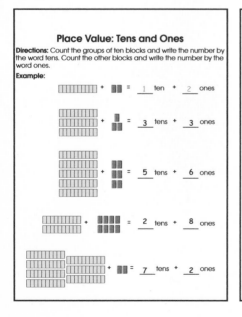

+ = 1 ten + 2 ones

+ = 3 tens + 3 ones

+ = 5 tens + 6 ones

+ = 2 tens + 8 ones

+ = 7 tens + 2 ones

Page 243

Place Value: Tens and Ones

Directions: Write the answers in the correct spaces.

	tens	ones		
3 tens, 2 ones	3	2	=	32
3 tens, 7 ones	3	7	=	37
9 tens, 1 one	9	1	=	91
5 tens, 6 ones	5	6	=	56
6 tens, 5 ones	6	5	=	65
6 tens, 8 ones	6	8	=	68
2 tens, 8 ones	2	8	=	28
4 tens, 9 ones	4	9	=	49
1 ten, 4 ones	1	4	=	14
8 tens, 2 ones	8	2	=	82
4 tens, 2 ones	4	2	=	42

28 = 2 tens, 8 ones
64 = 6 tens, 4 ones
56 = 5 tens, 6 ones
72 = 7 tens, 2 ones
38 = 3 tens, 8 ones
17 = 1 ten, 7 ones
63 = 6 tens, 3 ones
12 = 1 ten, 2 ones

Page 244

Review: Place Value

The place value of each digit, or numeral, is shown by where it is in the number. For example, in the number **123**, **1** has the place value of **hundreds**, **2** is **tens** and **3** is **ones**.

Directions: Count the groups of crayons and add.

Example:

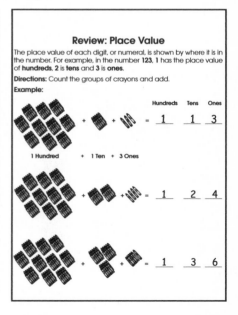

	Hundreds	Tens	Ones
+ + =	1	1	3

1 Hundred + 1 Ten + 3 Ones

+ + = 1 2 4

+ + = 1 3 6

Page 245

Counting by Fives
Directions: Count by fives to draw the path to the playground.

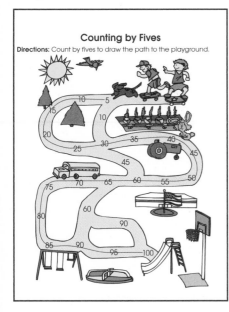

Page 246

Counting by Fives
Directions: Use tally marks to count by fives. Write the number next to the tallies.
Example: A tally mark stands for one = I. Five tally marks look like this = ⊞

⊞	5	⊞⊞⊞⊞⊞⊞⊞	35
⊞⊞	10	⊞⊞⊞⊞⊞⊞⊞⊞	40
⊞⊞⊞	15		45
⊞⊞⊞⊞	20		
⊞⊞⊞⊞⊞	25		50
⊞⊞⊞⊞⊞⊞	30		

Page 247

Counting by Tens
Directions: Count in order by tens to draw the path the boy takes to the store.

Page 248

Counting by Tens
Directions: Use the groups of 10's to count to 100.

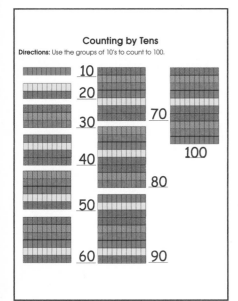

10, 20, 30, 40, 50, 60, 70, 80, 90, 100

Page 249

Addition: 10-15
Directions: Circle groups of ten crayons. Add the remaining ones to make the correct number.

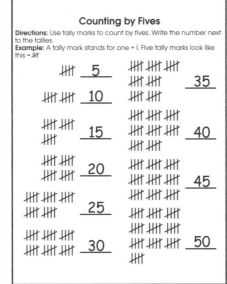

		tens	ones
	+	3	9
	+	5	7
	+	4	6
	+	6	7
	+	7	8
	+	9	6

6+6= 12   8+4= 12   9+5= 14

Page 250

Subtraction: 10-15
Directions: Count the crayons in each group. Put an **X** through the number of crayons being subtracted. How many are left?

		-		=	
		-	5	=	10
		-	4	=	7
		-	7	=	6
		-	6	=	8
		-	5	=	7
		-	8	=	6

13 - 8 = 5   11 - 5 = 6   12 - 9 = 3
14 - 7 = 7   10 - 7 = 3   13 - 3 = 10
15 - 9 = 6   11 - 8 = 3   12 - 10 = 2

Answer Key

343

Total Basic Skills Grade 1

Page 251

Shapes: Square

A square is a figure with four corners and four sides of the same length. This is a square □.

Directions: Find the squares and circle them.

Directions: Trace the word. Write the word.

square   square

Page 252

Shapes: Circle

A circle is a figure that is round. This is a circle ○.

Directions: Find the circles and put a square around them.

Directions: Trace the word. Write the word.

circle   circle

Page 253

Shapes: Square and Circle

Directions: Practice drawing squares. Trace the samples and make four of your own.

Directions: Practice drawing circles. Trace the samples and make four of your own.

Page 254

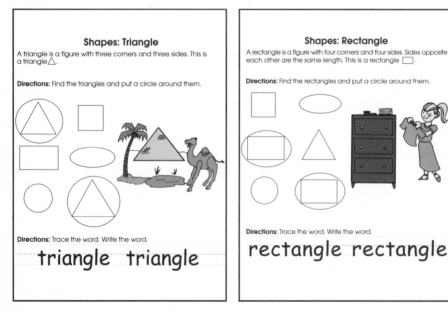

Shapes: Triangle

A triangle is a figure with three corners and three sides. This is a triangle △.

Directions: Find the triangles and put a circle around them.

Directions: Trace the word. Write the word.

triangle   triangle

Page 255

Shapes: Rectangle

A rectangle is a figure with four corners and four sides. Sides opposite each other are the same length. This is a rectangle ▭.

Directions: Find the rectangles and put a circle around them.

Directions: Trace the word. Write the word.

rectangle rectangle

Page 256

Shapes: Triangle and Rectangle

Directions: Practice drawing triangles. Trace the samples and make four of your own.

Directions: Practice drawing rectangles. Trace the samples and make four of your own.

Page 257

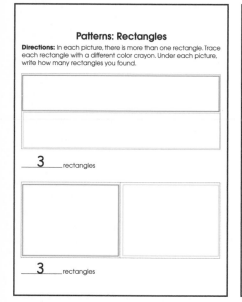

Patterns: Rectangles

Directions: In each picture, there is more than one rectangle. Trace each rectangle with a different color crayon. Under each picture, write how many rectangles you found.

___3___ rectangles

___3___ rectangles

Page 258

Patterns: Triangles

Directions: In each picture there is more than one triangle. Trace each triangle with a different color crayon. Under each picture, write how many triangles you found.

___2___ triangles

___3___ triangles

___2___ triangles

Page 259

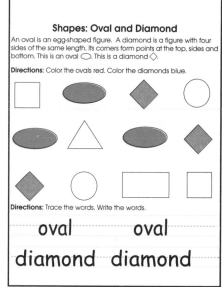

Shapes: Oval and Diamond

An oval is an egg-shaped figure. A diamond is a figure with four sides of the same length. Its corners form points at the top, sides and bottom. This is an oval ◯. This is a diamond ◇.

Directions: Color the ovals red. Color the diamonds blue.

Directions: Trace the words. Write the words.

oval   oval

diamond   diamond

Page 260

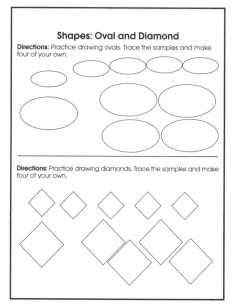

Shapes: Oval and Diamond

Directions: Practice drawing ovals. Trace the samples and make four of your own.

Directions: Practice drawing diamonds. Trace the samples and make four of your own.

Page 261

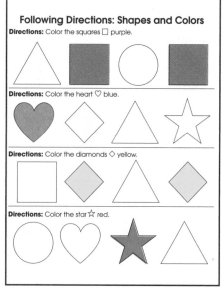

Following Directions: Shapes and Colors

Directions: Color the squares ☐ purple.

Directions: Color the heart ♡ blue.

Directions: Color the diamonds ◇ yellow.

Directions: Color the star ☆ red.

Page 262

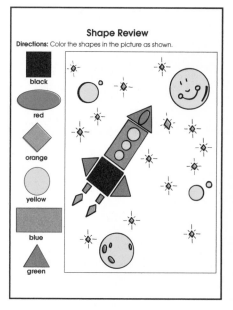

Shape Review

Directions: Color the shapes in the picture as shown.

black
red
orange
yellow
blue
green

Page 263

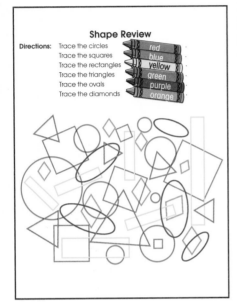

Shape Review

Directions: Trace the circles
Trace the squares
Trace the rectangles
Trace the triangles
Trace the ovals
Trace the diamonds

red
blue
yellow
green
purple
orange

Page 264

Classifying: Stars

Help Bob find the stars.

Directions: Color all the stars blue.

How many stars did you and Bob find? __10__

Page 265

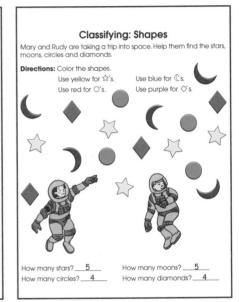

Classifying: Shapes

Mary and Rudy are taking a trip into space. Help them find the stars, moons, circles and diamonds.

Directions: Color the shapes.
Use yellow for ☆'s.   Use blue for ☾'s.
Use red for ○'s.   Use purple for ◇'s.

How many stars? __5__   How many moons? __5__
How many circles? __4__   How many diamonds? __4__

Page 266

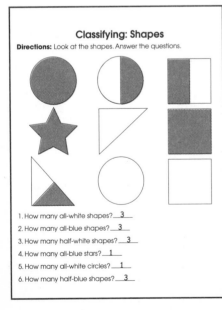

Classifying: Shapes

Directions: Look at the shapes. Answer the questions.

1. How many all-white shapes? __3__
2. How many all-blue shapes? __3__
3. How many half-white shapes? __3__
4. How many all-blue stars? __1__
5. How many all-white circles? __1__
6. How many half-blue shapes? __3__

Page 267

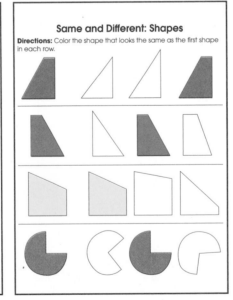

Same and Different: Shapes

Directions: Color the shape that looks the same as the first shape in each row.

Page 268

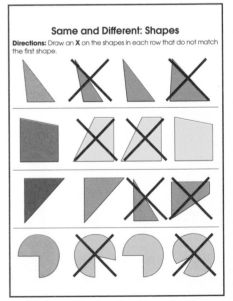

Same and Different: Shapes

Directions: Draw an **X** on the shapes in each row that do not match the first shape.

Page 269

Copying: Shapes and Colors

Directions: Color your circle to look the same.

Directions: Color your square to look the same.

Directions: Trace the triangle. Color it to look the same.

Directions: Trace the star. Color it to look the same.

Page 270

Copying: Shapes and Colors

Directions: Color the second shape the same as the first one. Then draw and color the shape two more times.

Page 271

Patterns: Shapes

Directions: Draw a line from the box on the left to the box on the right with the same shape and color pattern.

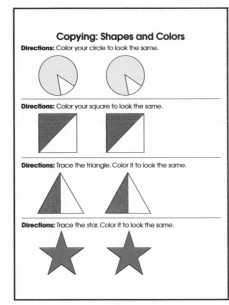

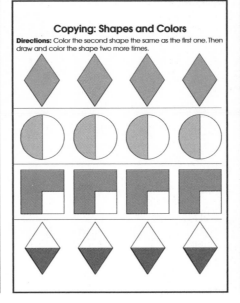

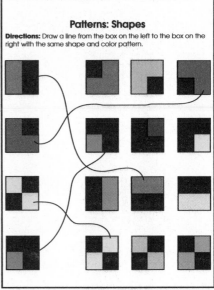

Page 272

Patterns: Shapes

Directions: Draw a line from the box on the left to the box on the right with the same shape and color pattern.

Page 273

Patterns: Find and Copy

Directions: Circle the shape in the middle box that matches the one on the left. Draw another shape with the same pattern in the box on the right.

Page 274

Patterns

Directions: Draw what comes next in each pattern.

Example:

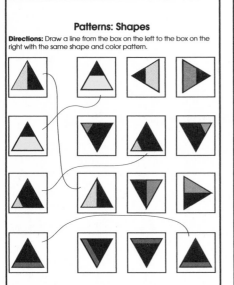

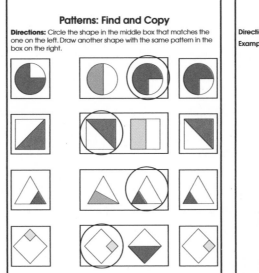

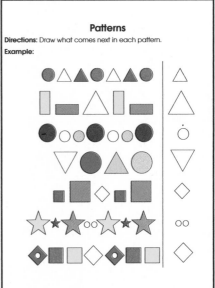

Page 275

Patterns

Directions: Fill in the missing shape in each row. Then color it.

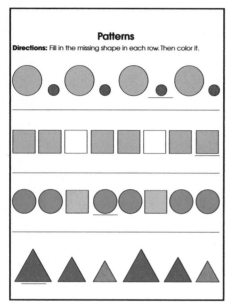

Page 276

Patterns

Directions: Color to complete the patterns.

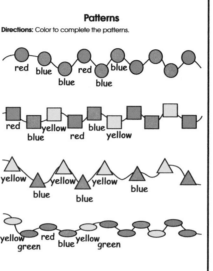

Page 277

Fractions: Whole and Half

A fraction is a number that names part of a whole, such as $\frac{1}{2}$ or $\frac{3}{4}$.

Directions: Color half of each object.

Example:

Whole apple   Half an apple

$$\frac{1}{2}$$

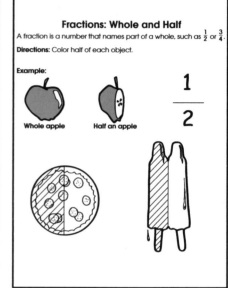

Page 278

Fractions: Halves $\frac{1}{2}$

$\frac{1}{2}$ Part shaded or divided / Number of equal parts

Directions: Color only the shapes that show halves.

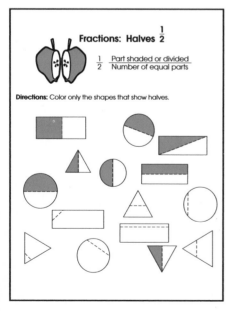

Page 279

Fractions: Thirds $\frac{1}{3}$

Directions: Circle the objects that have 3 equal parts.

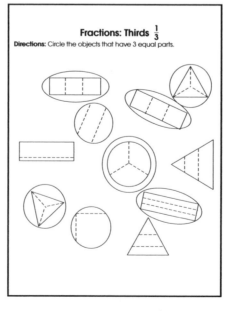

Page 280

Fractions: Fourths $\frac{1}{4}$

Directions: Circle the objects that have four equal parts.

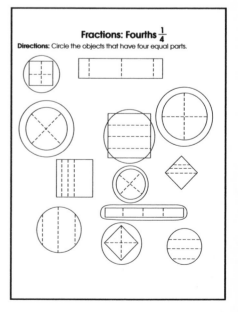

Page 281

Fractions: Thirds and Fourths

Directions: Each object has 3 equal parts. Color one section.

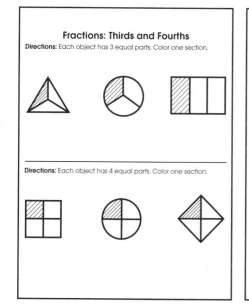

Directions: Each object has 4 equal parts. Color one section.

Page 282

Review: Fractions

Directions: Count the equal parts, then write the fraction.

Example:

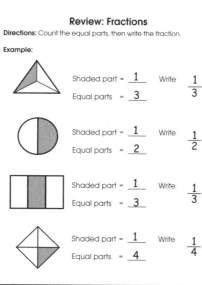

Shaded part = 1   Write $\frac{1}{3}$
Equal parts = 3

Shaded part = 1   Write $\frac{1}{2}$
Equal parts = 2

Shaded part = 1   Write $\frac{1}{3}$
Equal parts = 3

Shaded part = 1   Write $\frac{1}{4}$
Equal parts = 4

Page 283

Review

Directions: Write the missing numbers by counting by tens and fives.

_10_ , 20, _30_ , _40_ , _50_ , _60_ , 70, _80_ , _90_ , 100

5, _10_ , 15, _20_ , _25_ , 30, _35_ , _40_ , _45_ , _50_

Directions: Color the object with thirds red. Color the object with halves blue. Color the object with fourths green.

Directions: Draw a line to the correct equal part.

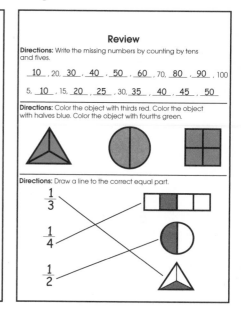

$\frac{1}{3}$

$\frac{1}{4}$

$\frac{1}{2}$

Page 284

Tracking: Straight Lines

Directions: Draw a straight line from A to B. Use a different color crayon for each line.

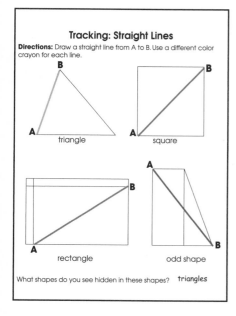

triangle   square

rectangle   odd shape

What shapes do you see hidden in these shapes?   **triangles**

Page 285

Tracking: Different Paths

Directions: Trace three paths from A to B.

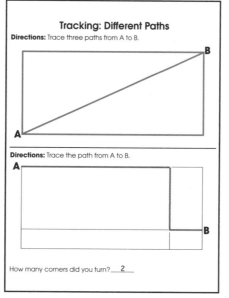

Directions: Trace the path from A to B.

How many corners did you turn? _2_

Page 286

Tracking: Different Paths

Help Megan find Mark.

Directions: Trace a path from Megan to Mark.

Paths may vary.

How many different paths can she follow to reach him? _8_

Page 287

Tracking: Different Paths

Directions: Use different colors to trace three paths the bear could take to get the honey.

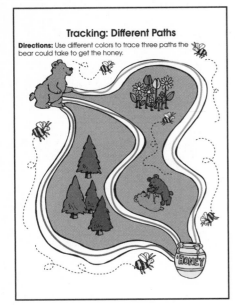

Page 288

Time: Hour

The short hand of the clock tells the hour. The long hand tells how many minutes after the hour. When the minute hand is on the **12**, it is the beginning of the hour.

Directions: Look at each clock. Write the time.

Example:

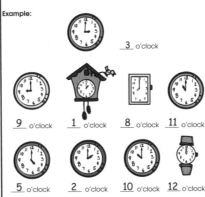

_3_ o'clock

_9_ o'clock   _1_ o'clock   _8_ o'clock   _11_ o'clock

_5_ o'clock   _2_ o'clock   _10_ o'clock   _12_ o'clock

Page 289

Time: Hour, Half-Hour

The short hand of the clock tells the hour. The long hand tells how many minutes after the hour. When the minute hand is on the **6**, it is on the half-hour. A half-hour is thirty minutes. It is written **:30**, such as **5:30**.

Directions: Look at each clock. Write the time.

Example:

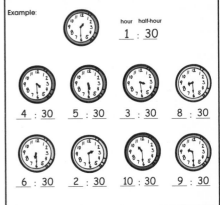

hour half-hour
_1_ : _30_

_4_ : 30   _5_ : 30   _3_ : 30   _8_ : 30

_6_ : 30   _2_ : 30   _10_ : 30   _9_ : 30

Page 290

Time: Hour, Half-Hour

Directions: Draw the hands on each clock to show the correct time.

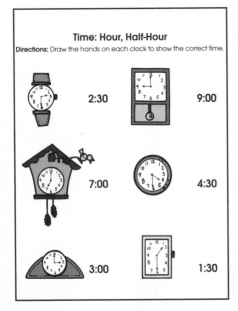

2:30   9:00

7:00   4:30

3:00   1:30

Page 291

Time: Counting by Fives

Directions: Fill in the numbers on the clock face. Count by fives around the clock.

There are 60 minutes in one hour.

Page 292

Time: Review

Directions: Look at the time on the digital clocks and draw the hands on the clocks.

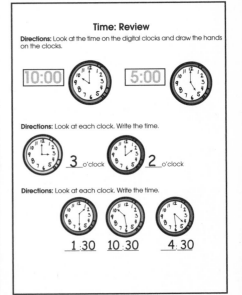

10:00   5:00

Directions: Look at each clock. Write the time.

_3_ o'clock   _2_ o'clock

Directions: Look at each clock. Write the time.

1:30   10:30   4:30

Directions: Cut out the word squares below. Match them to the pictures that rhyme.

bat	peg	fog
fun	cap	wig
box	hen	lip

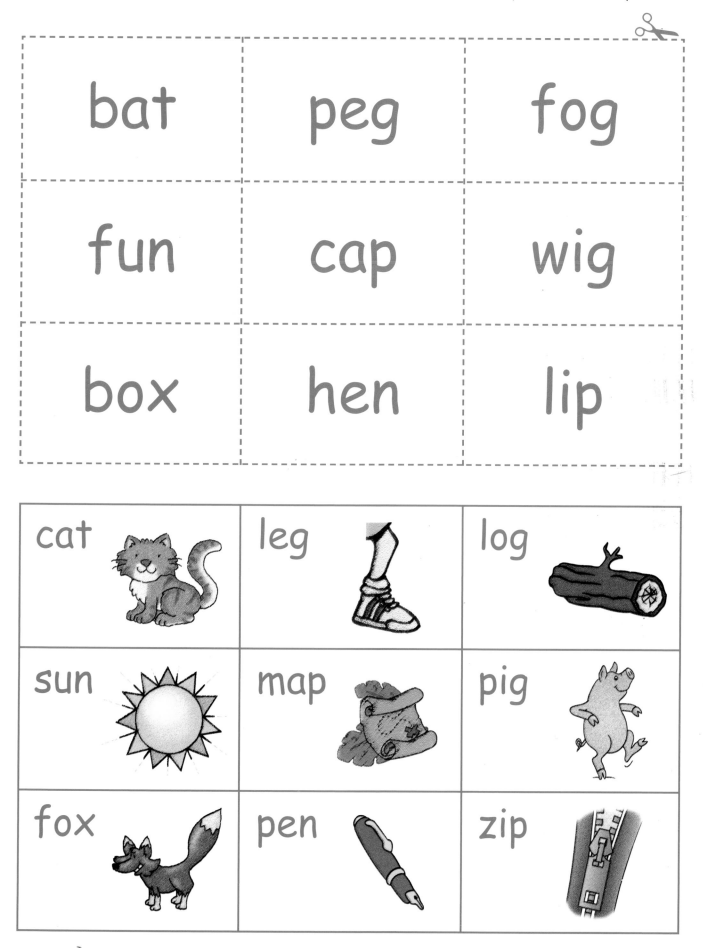

cat	leg	log
sun	map	pig
fox	pen	zip

Directions: Cut out the word squares below. Match them to the pictures that rhyme.

wing	pick	mess
tab	drink	man
wish	fix	cub

ring

brick

dress

crab

pink

van

fish

six

tub